80480

SOCIETY AND POWER

The University of Massachusetts Press
Amherst, 1977

Society and Power

Five New England Towns

1800–1860

Robert Doherty

Copyright © 1977 by Robert Doherty

All rights reserved

Library of Congress Catalog Card Number 77–73477

ISBN 0–87023–242–8

Printed in the United States of America

Designed by Mary Mendell

Library of Congress Cataloging in Publication Data

appear on the last printed page of the book

Contents

Preface

I BEGAN THIS BOOK several years ago in the hope that through detailed study I could come to some greater understanding of relationships between social change and behavior in Jacksonian America. More personally, I thought it would be fun to explore the possibilities of the then new conceptual and quantitative history. I had no firm idea as to where the project would go, what to look at, or how to handle the masses of data which I began gradually to accumulate. The study progressed, then, in more or less haphazard fashion.

I selected the communities to be studied primarily in terms of the availability of records and convenience to my home in Amherst, Massachusetts. However, in order to avoid problems of idiosyncrasy of findings, I wanted a variety of towns. I had no sure basis for knowing what that variety should represent, so I simply chose places that appeared to differ socially and economically from one another in both 1800 and 1860. If I could redo the study, I would not pick all the same towns for I now believe that central place and regional economic theory should be used as the basis for selection. Nevertheless, I think the towns studied here were diverse enough to offer comparative perspectives through which to test generalizations.

The project grew rapidly. It had no boundaries other than those imposed by my time, energy, and patience. My curiosity urged me continuously to extend the study. Each time I began to understand something, I realized that it was linked to something else and to something else beyond that. I often knew that there was other good evidence I could look at which would either confirm or wreck my hypotheses, but I also knew that the 3 or 4 pages I wanted to write about the subject were going to become 20 or perhaps 50 or perhaps more and that it would take a great deal of time to structure and analyze those new data. I frequently chose not to look at that new evidence even when I was quite sure it would pay off. When I had resolved in myself the quandaries which led me to begin this book, I felt that I should write down what I had found so I could move on. Otherwise, the project was simply going to be open ended and a lifetime's work.

I have not, then, so much finished this book as I have stopped writing it. What you see before you is a progress report which contains a variety of findings: hard data and firm generalizations, relationships in which connections range from strong to unproven, tentative but highly probable hypotheses, unproven hypotheses, along with several intuitive insights. As you read the book, you would do well to keep these various types of findings in mind. I hope all of them will hold up in the light of further research but frankly doubt if it will turn out that way. In any case, I will not be unhappy if others take up my ideas, examine them, and find them wrong. We will all learn something from that.

Many people have helped me to work out the ideas in this book. Ken Schueler, Joshua Chasan, and Dennis Kelly gave generously of their time in doing research. Walter Glazer, Jon Levine, Sam Hays, Mario DePillis, Ron Tobey, Irwin Flack, Stephan Thernstrom, Van Hall, Alfred Young, Richard Brown, and Julius Rubin have each read all or part of the manuscript, have offered encouragement, and have saved me from errors of judgment and fact. Peter Knights read the manuscript for the University of Massachusetts Press. He found several problems in logic and my use of data which I have corrected. The manuscript may still contain some errors for which I am responsible, but it is much improved as a result of Knights's reading.

I might never have finished this book without the generous support of the National Endowment for the Humanities, the American Association for State and Local History, the Labor Relations and Research Center of the Commonwealth of Massachusetts, and the University of Pittsburgh Faculty Research Committee.

Finally, it has been a pleasure working with the members of the staff at the University of Massachusetts Press in the preparation of this book for publication. They have been consistently helpful, prompt, and straightforward. Malcolm Call was unusually prompt and open during the period when the manuscript was under consideration, and Barbara Palmer helped make the book more literate with her editorial suggestions.

SOCIETY AND POWER

Major Railroads in Southern New England, 1860

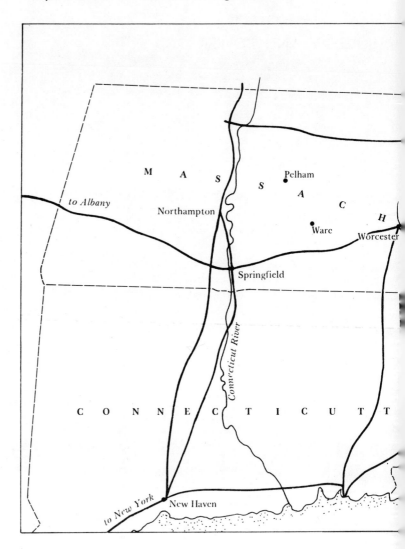

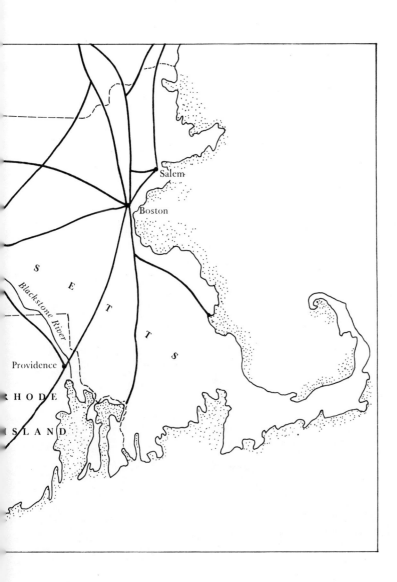

Salem

Boston

S

E

T

T

S

Blackstone River

Providence

RHODE

ISLAND

≈§ 1 ह≈

American Society

1800–1860: THEMES AND PROBLEMS

IN A NARROW SENSE, the book you are about to read is simply a study of how and why five communities in Massachusetts changed during the first half of the nineteenth century. But the book's themes relate to issues that are crucial to understanding the nature of antebellum society in the northern United States. This first chapter focuses on these themes and what other historians have written about them.

Because they contain an extraordinary and fascinating diversity, the volatile years between 1800 and 1860 have been the subject of repeated historical study. The diversity was really quite remarkable. Intellectual and artistic activity burst forth both among an elite and at the folk level. Prompted by a widened franchise and party organizations, politics emerged in a relatively modern form. New religious techniques and ideas tore at traditional churches, sponsored a far-reaching evangelical impulse, and promoted unique denominational forms. Troubled by change and sure that "things could be better," Americans organized themselves in an effort to remake society, or at least parts of it. Some of these re-formers reached out boldly to explore human potentiality at Walden, Oneida, and elsewhere, while others occupied themselves with more mundane matters, but wherever there were "problems" someone was bound to be trying to do something about them.

Ferment in literature, art, politics, religion, and reform does not exhaust the age's diversity, for major socioeconomic changes took place too. Foremost among them were westward migration and the so-called transportation revolution. In 1820 Americans had just begun to settle the continent, but by 1860 they had pushed from the Ohio Valley all the way to the Pacific Ocean and peopled most of the area in between. An ever-widening and more efficient transportation system of turnpikes, canals, railroads, and steamboat lines quickly linked these new lands with the east and crisscrossed through previously settled areas until much of the northern part of the country had been brought together as a marketplace. Businessmen responded with new, more complex systems of organization and production and, by the 1840s, the northeast had undergone rapid urbanization.

No matter where one looks—religion, politics, the economy—major qualitative changes were taking place; reason enough for historical curiosity about the epoch. However, the real source of fascination lies not simply in studying a variety of interesting but discrete events and changes but rather in trying to determine how apparently unrelated phenomena were in fact linked. From the very outset, historians have had in Alexis de Tocqueville's *Democracy in America* a set of ideas— an interpretive framework—which seems to show how disparate aspects of American thought, behavior, and society were tied together. Though Tocqueville made several serious errors, his *Democracy in America* remains the most comprehensive and provocative analysis of Jacksonian America. We will nevertheless have to modify Tocqueville's ideas in the light of recent research in order to identify the central issues and themes for the study of the five Massachusetts towns.

Tocqueville described America as an open society in which traditional European restraints of powerful church and state and inherited social position were absent. Born free of history, Americans existed as unattached individuals who could make whatever they willed of their lives. In the flux of competition, individual careers rose and fell, but most men remained of a middling sort and no inherited rich or poor class was to be found.

Americans paid a price for this unstructured society. Isolated and unprotected men turned to social conformity to mask their uncertainties. Individual freedom produced a timorous acquiescence to majority opinion. Nor could Americans rest on their achievements— they had to show off newly won attainments and to struggle continuously to avoid slipping back. Restlessly striving and insecure materialists resulted. Men who could not stop achieving—men who deferred to the majority and banded together in voluntary groups to gain objectives unavailable to their independent selves.

Tocqueville suggests that there are two keys to understanding relationships among the disparate aspects of Jacksonian society: social structure and a modal personality type or value system. Studies of American values and ideas by Leo Marx, John William Ward, and

Marvin Meyers have shown Tocqueville to have been essentially correct in his emphasis on individualism, achievement, competition, insecurity, materialism, equality, and disdain for tradition. Though often mutually contradictory, such values were powerful stimuli to change and experimentation. Put people with these sorts of values in an open, relatively unstructured society of the sort described by Tocqueville, and it is no wonder that an extraordinary outpouring of human spirit and energy took place.[1]

But was Tocqueville right about the nature of American social structure? How open was it? Did people really move up and down rapidly? Was opportunity there for the taking? Were most men of a middling sort? Was society largely without rich and poor? Were there no elites who dominated wealth and power throughout the period? In short, just how fluid was antebellum American society?

Since the early 1960s, historians have systemically studied American society, but the answers to these questions are unclear and sometimes contradictory. We do not yet have a comprehensive understanding of this nation's social structure, but it is important to review what we do already know so that crucial themes and problems may be identified.

The most striking discovery of recent social research is the astounding frequency with which Americans moved from one place to another. In his study of Boston, Massachusetts, Peter Knights discovered "incredible fluidity." Between 1850 and 1860, 61% of the heads of households in Knights's sample moved out of the city. During each ten-year period from 1830 to 1860, more than one-half of the household heads left Boston. Knights suggests that in the 1880s about one Bostonian in seven left the city each year but enough others moved in to produce a net population increase. He estimates that some 800,000 persons flowed in and out of Boston even though the city's 1890 population was only 448,000. Even more people moved within the city (about 30% annually changed their addresses). In any given year, then, about 14% of the population moved out of town, 30% moved within the city, while enough newcomers entered to compensate for the 14% loss and produce net population growth.[2]

These astounding rates of mobility were not unique to Boston. Despite variations from place to place, movement was consistently at high levels. In Newburyport, Massachusetts, 80% of the men listed in an 1849 city directory had disappeared by 1879. In Rochester, New York, 80% left between 1849 and 1859 while 70% departed Poughkeepsie, New York, between 1850 and 1860 and 40% left Omaha, Nebraska, between 1880 and 1883.

After reviewing such figures, Stephan Thernstrom and Peter Knights wonder:

> If American city-dwellers were as restless and footloose as our evidence suggests, how was any cultural continuity—or even the appearance of it maintained? . . . American society in the period under consideration here was more like a procession (with people flowing rapidly through it) than a stable social order. How did this social order cohere at all?

Howard Chudacoff in his study of Omaha writes that he believes mobility was so high as to preclude creation of social attachment. Thernstrom and Knights even raise the possibility of a class of unattached floaters or permanent transients.[3]

The larger meaning of widespread geographic mobility remains to be seen, but the initial impression is one of extraordinary flux: a society composed of restless individuals whose frequent moves cut them off from communal ties and freed them from such traditional restraints as gossip, family, and neighborhood.

Geographic mobility has often been viewed as disruptive of primary human ties—as a negative, alienating influence which destroys community and stimulates impersonal social arrangements. Most recent historians have avoided such an interpretation without necessarily disavowing it, but Rowland Berthoff has suggested that mobility was so "excessive" as to destroy social cohesion and usher in an age of disorder. According to Berthoff, nineteenth-century America is best understood as embodying a struggle to maintain stability in the face of overpowering forces of instability. Here is flux in the extreme, a society coming apart at the seams. And here too is the first set of crucial issues to be examined in this book: How much geographic mobility took place? Did mobility increase between 1800 and 1860? Who moved and who stayed? Why did they move? Was mobility "excessive" enough to overwhelm the social order and usher in an age of relative chaos?[4]

In his study of the *Discovery of the Asylum in America*, David Rothman suggests that Jacksonians were very much aware of disorder in their midst. Jacksonians, he argues, lived with a sense of peril that mobility, urbanization, and a breakdown of hierarchical social arrangements threatened to plunge the Republic into chaos. Fluidity and grandiose ambition destroyed family cohesion and communal solidarity and left criminals, paupers, and lunatics in their wake.[5]

Lest society really break apart, some Jacksonians set about creating institutions—prisons, insane asylums, and poorhouses—where discipline and order could be restored. These institutions would remove vulnerable individuals from the trauma of social flux, instill a sense of obedience and discipline, and enforce a commitment to hard work.

Rothman never precisely identifies the builders and caretakers of these institutions but describes them as "eminent and successful men." Nor does he investigate their motives for constructing means of confining and controlling social deviants. However, both Michael Katz, in his study of Massachusetts schools, and Raymond Mohl, in his examination of poor relief in New York City, argue that new institutions allowed members of the upper classes to control and manipulate persons in lower social strata and to imbue them with values congenial to upper-class interests in the new social order. Institutions fostered the docile, disciplined labor force necessary in the more complex urban economy of the 1840s and 1850s.[6]

Institutionalization did not stop with schools, prisons, poorhouses, and asylums but extended to many areas of society where increases in scale and complexity demanded more efficient organization. Politics, business, and voluntary associations all became increasingly rationalized as they began to develop bureaucratic and hierarchical structures so familiar to us today.

Since they were not bound to any one locale, many of these new structures conducted activities over a wide geographic scope. Furthermore, they were task oriented wherever their activities took them. Thus they sought to turn a profit, promote Bible reading, abolish slavery, or produce an electoral majority as efficiently as possible without much concern for local welfare and communal solidarity.[7]

Recent studies of wealth distribution and social stratification bear a much more ambiguous relationship to Tocquevillean flux than does research on institutionalization and geographic mobility. The Tocquevillean view of America holds that Americans were of a "middling sort" and that there was no ongoing wealthy elite, but current studies of wealth distribution have repeatedly found highly unequal ownership of property. Edward Pessen has shown that in large eastern cities the richest 1% of the population consistently owned more than 40% of the wealth. In 1845, the richest 4% in New York City owned about 80% of the property. Stuart Blumin found comparable inequities in Philadelphia where, in 1860, 10% of the men owned 89% of the wealth and the wealthiest 1% held about 50%. However, Merle Curti's study of the largely rural Trempealeau County, Wisconsin, shows the richest 10% of the property owners holding about 39% of the wealth, so it appears possible that ownership was more equitable in areas outside urban-commercial centers.[8]

Apparently, then, a society of relative economic equals existed only in rural or less developed areas. But the issue is not quite that simple. Imagine, for example, a society in which all people began their lives as equals and achieved at an equal rate. Inequality would result, for some people would be just starting to accumulate wealth while others would have been building their holdings for many years. Achievement produces inequality, and in such an open society wealth ownership would be a function of age. We know that young people went to cities in large numbers. Thus, skewed urban wealth distributions may be primarily a consequence of an urban age structure in which young adults predominated. A second set of issues emerges. How was wealth distributed? How were distributions related to economic activity and innovation, and were equitable distributions to be found only in less developed areas? To what extent did wealth ownership reflect not equality but an open society given to achievement in which ownership was essentially a function of age?

In an open society composed of people of a middling sort, it would also be expected that there would be no great fortunes, that elites would be unstable, that entry into wealthy groups would be relatively easy, and that the same wealthy groups would not long dominate power (i.e., that power would circulate among groups). Edward Pessen found an opposite tendency in eastern seaboard cities: a stable rich class which was difficult to enter. He discovered that most of Boston's rich in 1848 had either been rich 15 years before or had been members of the city's affluent families. Seventy-five percent of the men worth $50,000 in 1848 had been among the richest 2½% of the population in 1833. Comparable conditions existed in New York City, where 76% of the city's most affluent citizens in 1845 had been rich 17 years before. Pessen concludes that "the pursuit of wealth in the antebellum decades was marked not by fluidity but by stability."[9]

This stable rich group wielded considerable power. Most municipal political offices were held by affluent merchants, lawyers, financiers, and businessmen. The very rich did not often run for election, but a second level of well-to-do men prevailed and their influence was not seriously challenged from below by manufacturers or any other group. The most notable change found by Pessen was an increase of artisan officeholders, but they occupied only about 10% of the positions in Boston, New York, and Philadelphia between 1838 and 1850.[10]

Pessen's findings on elite continuity and power are somewhat surprising since they seem to contradict other theories about elite behavior during the decades prior to the Civil War. Many historians have argued that old elites declined and that their status and power were threatened by new manufacturing groups. Robert Dahl discovered that in New Haven, Connecticut, new entrepreneurs drove old elites from local political power in the 1840s. Other historians—Clifford Griffin, David Donald, George M. Frederickson—have indicated that established elites suffered from a "loss of status" as new groups rose to wealth. In response, members of old elites turned to voluntary activities, reform, personal exploration and challenge, literature, art, and military service in order to maintain social influence and power and to promote continued meaning in their lives.[11]

Here is a third set of issues to be examined. How successful were members of older elites? Did they prosper and, if so, how? Did they sustain their power and did new people rise to positions of influence? If power shifted hands, why and how did the shift occur? What relationships can be established between continuity of power and socioeconomic change?

Even if the very rich elites were relatively stable, a great deal of social mobility may have occurred in middling and lower social strata. In a study of vertical mobility among laborers in Newburyport, Massachusetts, between 1850 and 1880, Stephan Thernstrom did find considerable upward movement, but most moves were small and none was of a rags-to-riches variety. Between 1850 and 1860, 36% of Thernstrom's sample improved their occupations, and in the next decade several more made their way out of the ranks of the unskilled. Sons of unskilled workers were even more successful, for only 10% of them remained in their fathers' lowly trades between 1850 and 1870. Yet most mobility was only a small step up from unskilled to semi-skilled—hardly enough to suggest high fluidity.[12]

Property mobility was more readily available to Newburyport laborers than was occupational improvement. More than two-thirds of those who remained in town for as many as 20 years became owners of small amounts of real estate. But such gains were made at the cost of underconsumption and child labor and thus may have sacrificed future improvements for minimal present security. Children, for example, often worked rather than attending school and gave up opportunities to enter white-collar trades which required education.

An old, economically static community such as Newburyport was certainly unrepresentative of American society in general, but Thernstrom's findings hold up reasonably well in other settings. Stuart Blumin's study of mobility in Philadelphia between 1820 and 1860 shows interdecadal occupational improvement among semiskilled and unskilled laborers to have been about 30%. However, Philadelphia workers more often climbed to skilled and nonmanual trades than did their counterparts in Newburyport.[13]

What of mobility among middling social strata where we might expect movement to have been most common? Herbert Gutman has demonstrated that large social and economic gains were made by manufacturers and metal workers in Paterson, New Jersey, between 1830 and 1880. Gutman argues that most successful manufacturers in Paterson had started their careers as workingmen and that the rags-to-riches promise was very real in this one rapidly expanding city, where manufacturing did not require large amounts of initial capital.[14]

Blumin's data on Philadelphia are not strictly comparable to Gutman's since Gutman looked only at the social origins of the successful while Blumin examined the whole population. Still, Blumin found much less upward mobility in middle social strata than Gutman's work on Paterson would lead us to expect. But Blumin also discovered considerable downward movement among this same population, so persons of a middling sort did move up and down a great deal. Nevertheless, their movement up and down did not equal that of laborers.

What are we to make of these studies of social mobility and their seemingly contradictory findings? No firm conclusions appear justified, but at least key questions and a fourth set of issues can be identified. How much vertical mobility took place? Who succeeded and who did not? Did vertical mobility adhere to the pattern of relative stability and incremental movement at the top and bottom and volatility in middle strata which the work of Pessen, Thernstrom, and Gutman might suggest? Or was Blumin more nearly correct in his assertion that as society became more stratified between 1800 and 1860 opportunity was increasingly difficult to find? Of course a larger possibility exists here that mobility was a function of economic and social context. For the most part, Blumin, Thernstrom, Pessen, and Gutman studied mobility in different sorts of places. Perhaps variations in their conclusions are simply a product of variations in the places they studied. Here, then, is a crucial issue to be examined in this study of Massachusetts towns. What was the influence of place or socioeconomic context on social mobility?

Study of four key issues seems to promise greater understanding of American social structure between 1800 and 1860:

1. *Geographic mobility.* How much mobility took place, and did it increase between 1800 and 1860? Who moved and who stayed? Why did people move? Was mobility "excessive" enough to overwhelm the social order and usher in an age of relative chaos?

2. *Distribution of wealth.* How equally was wealth distributed? How were distributions related to economic activity and innovation, and were equitable distributions to be found only in less developed areas? To what extent did wealth distributions reflect not equality but an open society, given to achievement, in which ownership was primarily a function of age?

3. *Power and political continuity.* How successful were members of old dominant groups? Did they prosper and, if so, how? Did they sustain their political power, or did new men rise to positions of influence? If power did change hands, how did the shift take place, and how was it related to overall socioeconomic change?

4. *Social (vertical) mobility.* How much vertical mobility took place? Who succeeded and who did not? Did vertical mobility adhere to a pattern of relative stability and incremental movement at the top and bottom of society and volatility in the middle? What was the influence of place or socioeconomic context on social mobility?

In seeking the answers to these questions, we would like to discover the level of openness or fluidity in American society during the middle of the nineteenth century. But fluidity and openness are ambiguous and value-laden terms. We had better define them more precisely. Openness implies a morally good society in which men exercised substantial control over their lives—a society in which they were free to choose from among several careers and life styles. Many of the participants in this good, open society would have attained material and psychological security. Free from anxieties about basic necessities and certain about the integrity and worth of their own selves, they would have had the capacity to live vital and fulfilling lives. Seen in this way, openness implies widespread availability of material and emotional security, the presence of alternatives, and the opportunity to gain a sense of personal worth.

Unfortunately, lack of data prevents us from examining the psychological dimensions of openness, so we must be content with a much narrower focus upon the issues of choice and material security. Though our arguments may often appear to stray, we will continuously try to answer a single set of interrelated questions: To what extent were people able to attain material security and make choices about their lives? Which social and economic factors appear to have contributed to the availability of choice and security?

ఆ§ 2 *§ఴ*

The Five Towns

FIVE TOWNS IN MASSACHUSETTS form the basis for this study: Pelham, Ware, Northampton, Worcester, and Salem. In 1800, these five communities represented three different types of places: hilltowns (Ware and Pelham), market and administrative centers (Northampton and Worcester), and a major international seaport (Salem). Each type of town will be described in turn.[1]

Hilltowns (Ware and Pelham)

As the name implies, the hilltowns were located in the hilly regions of west central Massachusetts. Undesirable as they were for farming, their uneven terrain and stony, unproductive soil did not attract settlers until the late eighteenth century. Nor did settlers come in large numbers, for life was hard and a meager subsistence agriculture prevailed. In 1800 Pelham contained 1,144 people and Ware, 997. A few hilltown farmers raised sheep and traded potash and charcoal with outsiders, but most cultivated only a few acres and struggled to avoid poverty. Because they were devoid of opportunity, no extended commercial activity took place in the hilltowns, so local residents had little chance to accumulate capital or to acquire complex business skills. Without commerce, neither Ware nor Pelham developed a center containing more than a few ill-kept buildings. Sparsely settled and composed of widely scattered unprosperous farms, Ware and Pelham never fit the classic New England pattern of a town center, stores, church, a green, and outlying farms. Bound to subsistence agriculture, north of east-west transportation routes, and isolated by the hills, Pelham and Ware remained cut off from the outside world. They were, in short, highly provincial places.

Market and Administrative Centers
(Northampton and Worcester)

Old and prosperous, Northampton and Worcester formed economic and political centers for hinterlands stretching out several miles from their boundaries. Their populations in 1800 were about twice those of the hilltowns (Northampton, 2,190; Worcester, 2,411). Lawyers and judges built homes in these county seats as did other public officials and newspaper publishers. Newspapers continuously appeared in these thriving towns from 1800 until 1860. Inns and taverns grew up around the courthouses and on the many roads which ran to other towns and cities and meandered out into rural hinterlands. Merchants used these roads and the Connecticut River in Northampton to foster an extensive trade so that the two communities became important points of distribution between large urban centers like Boston and the rural interior. Worcester and Northampton were two of the most significant such secondary commercial centers in early nineteenth-century Massachusetts. A contemporary describes Worcester in 1793:

> within a compass of one mile, and mostly on one street, are collected the county officers, a number of merchants and shop-keepers, professional men, and mechanics of various sorts. A very great trade is carried on here in European and West India goods; and the adjacent county is supplied from this town; here are apothecary stores, and stores of all kinds of hardware. . . . [Worcester is] one of the most populous, lively, flourishing, agreeable inland places in the state.[2]

Commercial, legal, and administrative opportunity stimulated growth of town centers until both Northampton and Worcester had small villages with shops, homes, and taverns spread around central greens where church and courthouse stood. Many well-to-do and cosmopolitan men lived in these villages—men interested in the wider world who had the experience and capital necessary to operate large-scale economic ventures. Artisans—blacksmiths, shoemakers, and the like—also populated the villages, and even though they never attained the wealth of the judges, lawyers, and merchants, many of them seem to have gained a comfortable living.

A short distance from these small but flourishing town centers, prosperous farms could be found. Northampton farmers tilled some of the very best land in New England and often owned large flocks of sheep. Though self-sufficient farming predominated, commercial agriculture could be found as early as the seventeenth century and remained profitable enough to allow some Northampton farmers to accumulate large amounts of property. Lacking the superior soil and river transportation available in Northampton, Worcester agriculturists cultivated smaller plots and found fewer commercial opportunities than did farmers in the Connecticut Valley. But Worcester farmers worked good land which brought them solid security and some surpluses. A few Worcester husbandmen were quite well off.

In comparison with the hilltowners, people in the administrative and market centers were much more prosperous and had many more connections with the outside. They lived in communities with better land and transportation, where commercial opportunities could be found. Among the residents of the administrative-market centers were a few men of wealth, experience, and broad personal ties, men who could promote economic development in the nineteenth century.

International Seaport (Salem)

On the seacoast about 15 miles north of Boston, highly urbanized Salem was physically smaller than the other four towns. Most of her 9,457 citizens lived on a small, densely populated neck of land—an area of approximately 300 acres, which was about one mile long and between one-half and one-quarter mile wide. Roughly 900 dwelling houses were jammed together, intermixed with about 650 outbuildings and 400 or so shops, ropewalks, sail lofts, and other buildings. Along the waterfronts were wharves, warehouses, and counting rooms, but generally little geographic specialization had taken place and economic activities were widely intermixed with residential housing. Nevertheless, ropewalks and tanneries had begun to locate on one side of town east of the commons, and on Federal and Chestnut streets well-to-do merchants had started to map out more exclusive places to live.

Salem took in about 2,000 acres outside this small urbanized area. These lands presented several aspects: islands, swamps, meadows, and grasslands. A few people lived out on these properties, some of these acres were farmed, but the core of Salem lay on the neck near the sea.

A leading seaport and one of the nation's ten largest cities, Salem was at the height of a short-lived prosperity in 1800. The American Revolution had turned her sailors away from fishing, disrupted her trade, and forced some Tories into exile, but privateering and reborn initiative quickly filled whatever gaps there had been. Salem merchants had more than 200 vessels engaged in commerce in 1810 and had boldly opened new areas for American commerce. They dealt in hides and gum arabic from South America; sugar and molasses from the West Indies; wine from Madeira; ivory, gold dust, palm oil, peanuts, and camphorwood from Africa; silk, cotton, spices, sugar, and chinaware from China, India, and the Isle of France. The most important part of this trade lay in the East Indies where, for a time, Salem merchants monopolized the world trade in pepper and other spices.[3]

This far-flung and highly profitable commerce depended on the aggressiveness of Salem's merchants and a peculiar set of international conditions. Based almost entirely on overseas trade, Salem's activities brought few ties with the American interior. When the international situation changed and American economic activity turned inward, Salem merchants were ill equipped to compete. Despite her merchants' skills and experience, Salem's trade was largely taken over by Boston after 1815. With overseas commerce on the decline, Salem merchants never successfully penetrated the interior. But Salem's economy did not collapse after 1815. Profits could still be made in international commerce and the coasting trade in lumber, coal, hides, and cotton. Most wealthy and ambitious Salemites took themselves and their money to Boston, New York, and elsewhere, but some middle-level merchants stayed and kept Salem as a base for operations functioning out of other ports. Still others searched for new avenues of commerce with Salem as their home port or shifted their attention more toward banking, insurance, internal improvements, and manufacturing.

Probably the nation's richest community per capita in 1800, Salem contained several of the wealthiest men in America. Salem merchants attained prominence in national and state government and most members of the town's leading families were tied to regional New England elites. Here were some of the richest, most skillful, experienced, and best-connected men in the country, men who had both the resources and ability to direct economic development. But Salem itself did not fully benefit from this talent and experience since most of the great merchants left Salem to take up more extensive opportunities in Boston and New York.

Beneath these very rich men was a group of artisans and businessmen who attained economic success in their own right. Yet most of their work was linked to shipping and trade, either directly, as among shipbuilders and sailmakers, or indirectly, as was the case with coopers and tanners. Salem's wholehearted commitment to commerce thus tied the economic fate of these artisans to that of the merchants and put them in a situation of relative dependency. Below the artisans in the very bottom ranks of Salem society were poor and unskilled laborers—carters, fishermen, mariners, and the like. The great social and economic distance between these propertyless laborers and the merchants indicates the development of a highly stratified commercial society in Salem.

Bases for Variations among the Towns

Differences among the three types of towns appear to be the result of (1) the sort of economic activity which went on within them, especially the degree of commercial activity, and (2) the locus of the communities in a hierarchy of cities created by the regional marketplace or, in Salem, the location in the international economy. Hilltowns such as Ware and Pelham lay at the extreme bottom end of a tier of cities produced by a commercial network reaching out from Boston through Northampton and Worcester and on into the hilltowns. The scale and diversity of economic activity was severely restricted at the hilltown end of the network but increased in the market centers and top-level places such as Boston. Thus, as market centers and middle-level places, Northampton and Worcester contained more, and more extensive, activities than either Ware or Pelham, where subsistence agriculture prevailed except for one or two tiny stores. Located on especially desirable sites with good farm land, near rivers and other natural transportation routes, the market centers of Worcester and Northampton were settled early and, as well situated, established communities, were chosen as shire towns and county seats, thus encouraging further development and diversity.

Salem's prosperity depended on international trade. Her merchants carried goods from port to port all over the world but did not engage in internal commerce. Therefore, in many respects, Salem had no place at all in the commercial network described above. Salem's single-minded involvement in overseas trade generated great riches, but it also restricted diversity, cut off alternate opportunities, and produced a vertically organized economy and society in which the economic fate of everyone was tied to a single economic activity.

Core Population and Local Elites

In 1800, each of the five towns had a core population composed of long-resident local families. The three more commercial communities also contained economic elites, that is, rich and powerful men. The quality of core and elite and relationships between them influenced long-term development and such processes as social mobility and shifts in political power, so core and elite characteristics merit close attention.[4]

Families forming the core had lived in town two or more generations and/or were related to initial settlers. Members of such families frequently intermarried both in first marriages and as widows and widowers so that in older communities blood relationships could become so complex that a member of one core family was related in some fashion to members of all the rest. People belonging to these families stayed in town much more often than did other residents and formed a center of potential stability for town society as a whole.

In his study of Salem in 1800, Bernard Farber describes such core families as "guardians of virtue," who perpetuated Puritan traditions of a patriarchal and hierarchical community. But he also contends that family cohesion, continuity, and power were tied to economic circumstance and were maintained only among persons of middling station. Family influence broke down among the rich and poor.

Farber's ideas make considerable sense not simply for Salem but also for the other four towns. In Pelham and Ware, core families numbered about one-quarter of the heads of households, owned about one-third of each community's real estate, and occupied roughly one-half of the local political offices. But as subsistence farmers, they lacked the resources necessary to sustain family influence and power. Local opportunities were simply not great enough to encourage family solidarity beyond the nuclear unit. High birth rates and numerous children among the core families produced a population surplus for which there were few ongoing chances in Pelham and Ware. Property and inheritance could not be used to maintain solidarity. Nor, for that matter, could core members produce enough wealth or consensus to maintain a church continuously. Even the town meeting does not seem to have been an effective agency for sustaining family or communal solidarity. Under these circumstances, no economic elite appeared, and core influence in these two hilltowns was highly vulnerable to disruption, especially through penetration by affluent outsiders.

Two factors account for core weakness in the hilltowns. Settled as they were by individuals who lacked any common purpose, Pelham and Ware did not have a consensual tradition of the sort present in group-founded, covenanted New England towns. That is, they lacked social and intellectual traditions on which to base family solidarity and dominance in a hierarchically structured community. Nor did they have the material resources necessary to solidify extended kin ties or even to sustain parental influence over adult offspring.

Northampton and Worcester provided the sort of middling circumstances which Farber believes contributed to family solidarity. Furthermore, both towns had been founded under covenants and thus had powerful traditions of Puritan communality. Representing 40% of the heads of households, Northampton's large and complex core families owned more than one-half of the real estate, filled roughly three-quarters of the local political offices, and dominated the town's only church. Northampton core members could be found at all social levels except the very bottom, but most were congregated in middle strata and above. Northampton's very rich men—the elite—were members of core families, so in effect core and elite were one and no conflict appeared between them.

Core members in Northampton used their moderate wealth and ongoing local opportunity to perpetuate family ties. They passed family skills and property on to children and relatives as bequests at death, as gifts of land or money at age 25 or so, and as clerks and apprentices in an uncle's or cousin's store, shop, or law office. They also looked after poor and aged cousins, aunts, brothers and sisters-in-law and made sure that widows were provided for. Charles L. Seeger of Northampton sped his sons Edwin and Augustus toward success with gifts of $1,800 and $1,000 when they left home. Caleb Strong helped his daughters toward financial security with presents of money when they first married and a $13,000 bequest to be divided between them when he died. Joseph Lyman gave his son land in Northampton. Elias Lyman loaned his children money.

No doubt there were clashes within and between families but no evidence such as contested wills, lawsuits, and petty bickering could be found except for some religious disputes in the 1820s. Solidarity apparently prevailed because of convenanted traditions, the unity of core and elite, and the availability of moderate wealth and opportunity. Furthermore, since most core members had at least one close relative engaged in nonagricultural pursuits, they were potentially able to take advantage of new opportunities opening on or off the farm. Such opportunities, coupled with elaborate and continuing family ties and an absence of serious internal divisions, meant that Northampton's core families were well prepared to continue their influence and power into the nineteenth century.

Worcester's core families claimed 14.5% of the heads of households, 30% of the real estate, and 54% of the town's political offices between 1800 and 1810. Though similar traditions and economic circumstances prevailed in Worcester and Northampton, Worcester's core families were unable to perpetuate either their solidarity or their power. Because it was settled after Northampton, Worcester had not been populated by a few large families, nor had she had time to develop the extremely complex kin relationships found in the other market town. Nevertheless, Worcester had evolved much as had Northampton until it was torn apart by the American Revolution when many leading core members who were British loyalists were forced to flee.

Internally divided and deprived of many of its wealthier nonfarm leaders, Worcester's core solidarity was never reestablished. Rather, the core was split between town center and countryside. Business and professional men in the center, both core and noncore, joined with several wealthy entrepreneurs who had recently arrived from Boston and formed a new economic elite based on wealth, occupation, and economic connections rather than family ties. This elite, the wealthiest of whom were outsiders, formed a new (Unitarian) church and joined together in exclusive groups such as the Worcester Fire Society. Though composed of only 100 or so men, this nonfarm, center-based group dominated local politics between 1800 and 1830. Control by such a small group suggests that conflict between its members and other communal residents must have been small, for elite members had to stand for election each year and could only be chosen with support from outside their own group. Furthermore, most local elections appear to have been carried by large majorities between 1800 and 1810. Still, the division between core and elite remained.

Despite other similarities, Worcester's core and elite had evolved differently from Northampton's. In Northampton, the two groups cannot be distinguished since rich and successful farmers and nonfarmers were also members of core families. However, in Worcester, core and elite had separated, lessening the influence of family ties and allowing entry of wealthy outsiders to positions of influence and power. Worcester entered the nineteenth century under the dominance of a small group of nonfarmers who lived in the town's center and whose connections were based on economic ties and common values (witness the Unitarian Church) rather than on familial bonds.

Salem's core and elite developed in ways unlike any of the other four towns but more like Worcester than the other three. In 1800, Salem's core families, that is, those families descended from town founders and/or locally present for two or more generations, represented 11% of the heads of households, owned 23% of the real estate, and held 37% of the town offices between 1800 and 1810. But family

cohesion appears to have persisted only among middle-strata artisans; it had broken down among wealthier merchants.

Commercial rivalries, internal stresses in family business, struggles
over inheritance, and a relentless search for profit all divided Salem
merchants from one another and from their own kin. These internal
problems, coupled with the rise to wealth of new men like the Crowninshield brothers, caused the Salem economic elite to split into savagely warring rival factions whose conflicts penetrated all aspects of
elite activity—dancing assemblies, social clubs, religion, business,
politics, and even marriage. Because Salem's economy was so tied to
overseas trade, the merchants were able to coerce their employees and
artisans to join in factional dispute. Nearly every town resident was
forced to choose sides in the struggle for control of Salem among
members of the Derby and Crowninshield families between 1790 and
1805. Salem's mercantile elite was thus bitterly divided and these
divisions extended down to encompass the whole community.

Most of Salem's old families—the core—supported the Derby Fed-
eralist faction while newcomers joined the Crowninshields. Marriages
were usually within factional boundaries though important exceptions
such as the marriage of the founding patriarchs of the Derby and
Crowninshield families to each other's sisters ripped at family unity.
The tie between family and faction often produced incredibly petty
wrangles which quickly spread beyond the immediate disputants.

Dissipation of time, energy, and money in clandestine scheming,
punitive lawsuits, and the like contributed to the demise and splinter-
ing of leading elite families, but internal family politics had an equally
devastating impact. Family patriarchs—the initial moneymakers—
seem often to have produced sons who could not maintain the family
business. Once the patriarch died, heirs fought among themselves,
not just over the estate but also over business decisions. It was
common in Salem for family partnerships to place enormous strain on
the participants, and cohesion of extended families invariably lost out
to an increased solidarity of nuclear units.

Family politics disrupted extended kin ties while factional squab-
bling prevented development of a cohesive upper class. Both family
politics and factional discord also led many members of leading families to leave Salem. As supporters of the Derby Federalists, core
members were particularly inclined to flee when the Crowninshield
Republicans gained power after 1800. Divided within themselves,
given to factional bickering, subject to internal dispute, neither
Salem's elite nor its core families possessed much cohesion but increasingly functioned as separate nuclear units.

ৼৡ 3 ৡ৾

Economic Change
1800–1860

TRANSFORMED BY ECONOMIC and demographic changes, all of the towns, except for Pelham, had become very different sorts of places in 1860 from what they had been a half century before. Chapter 3 examines these changes first in the economy and then in the composition and distribution of town population. Emphasis is placed on differences among the towns so that we may better understand the impact of context on the social processes described in chapter 1.

Between 1800 and 1860, New Englanders built an extensive new transportation system. Beginning in the late eighteenth century with turnpikes, several thousand miles of new roads, canals, and railroads were constructed. Northampton and Worcester appeared to be early beneficiaries of this process as canals were dug connecting them with southern New England seaports. However, such benefits proved elusive, for these waterways soon lost their profits to an expanding network of railroads.[1]

Massachusetts and surrounding states had several thousand miles of railroads in operation by 1860, and New England had rail links extending throughout the northern United States. Construction in New England produced two major east-west routes (New York-New Haven-Boston and Boston-Worcester-Springfield-Albany) and several somewhat parallel north-south lines (e.g., the eastern seacoast, Providence-Worcester, Norwich-Worcester, Springfield-Northampton, New Haven-Springfield). As the main terminus of many lines, Boston extended her role as New England's most important city. But other cities such as Worcester, which were located on north-south and east-west rail junctions, benefited too and formed a level of cities second only to Boston in opportunity for diverse economic expansion. Astride several important rail lines and at the center of a rapidly growing hinterland, Worcester emerged as a major point of exchange whose commercial, financial, and legal business greatly expanded. Competition from Boston restricted Worcester's development to that of a secondary center, but within that limitation, Worcester boomed and diversified.

Towns at some distance from important junctions but still on north-south rail lines became third-level places which served small hinterlands but whose expansion was restricted by the superior facilities of the junction cities. Thus, Northampton slipped from a secondary to a tertiary place subject to the influence of Springfield, Massachusetts, the junction city 30 miles to the south.

Springfield possessed both north-south and east-west rail connections which allowed that city to evolve as a secondary center comparable to Worcester. Northampton was served only by a much less important north-south line so most goods had to be transshipped in Springfield to go north to Northampton. Springfield now became the most important city in western Massachusetts, usurping economic functions from other towns and dominating trade and transportation throughout the area. Unable to compete, Northampton slid toward lesser commercial status, serving the needs of a relatively small and slowly growing hinterland in Hampshire County.

Nor did Salem fare well, for her railroads were only spurs into the nearby interior and to north-south routes dominated by Boston. Prohibiting diversity of the sort found in Worcester, Boston's economic orbit reached past Salem and helped Bostonians to continue their takeover of Salem's economy. No longer a major seaport or city, Salem skidded toward an economic demise to be halted in the late 1840s by the rise of manufacturing. No transportation improvements, railroad or otherwise, came to Pelham or Ware, and they remained among the lowest in New England's hierarchy of cities.

This new hierarchy had four levels. At the top stood Boston. Just below were junction cities such as Worcester. Beneath the junction cities were market centers like Northampton, and at the bottom were rural hamlets such as Pelham and Ware. For the sake of convenience and clarity, we may designate these four types of communities as top-level, upper-level, middle-level, and lower-level places. These designations are important and should be remembered. They are used throughout the remainder of the book.

Transportation improvements rearranged old economic functions and produced new relationships among cities in which Worcester gained, Northampton and Salem lost, and Pelham and Ware remained about the same. What does this mean and why is it important?

Opportunities in commercial and service businesses are a function of location and were greater in upper-level places like Worcester than in middle-level ones such as Northampton. Operations at the upper level could be more diverse and larger than at the middle level. Substantial wholesale and retail establishments prospered in Worcester but could not in Northampton because the market was too small. In fact, wholesale merchants in the upper level (Worcester) supplied smaller traders at the middle level (Northampton) who in turn distributed goods to tiny stores in the lower level (Pelham). Transportation and its effects on an urban hierarchy determined the nature and quality of commercial and service opportunities, and as an expanding upper-level city, Worcester offered chances for economic gain which could not be found in the other four towns.

Transportation improvements throughout the east and midwest altered opportunities in the production of goods as well as their sale. Railroads created a vastly enlarged and more complex market in which goods made in New England could be sold throughout the United States but had to compete with products from other parts of the country. Since they were protected from outside competition by slow and expensive transportation, producers in the past had been largely restricted to a noncompetitive local market, but now both protection and restrictions were lifted except for bulky or perishable goods. Cheap transportation meant each place and each producer could compete with all the rest.

The advent of canals and railroads had an especially strong effect on agriculture. Food staples from New York and the midwest penetrated New England markets and forced local farmers to concentrate on products which could not be profitably shipped long distances. Such changes did not destroy agricultural opportunities, for the growth of cities in New England offered an expanding market for perishables. Farmers in the four agricultural towns shifted toward market-oriented products. Most husbandmen remained essentially self-sufficient, but they also began to produce hay, dairy products, butter, cheese, meat, apples, and vegetables for sale in nearby communities. Some agriculturists even became primarily commercial, with their activities closely keyed to the marketplace. Agriculture generally benefited from these new conditions, but hilltown farmers probably made the greatest relative gains. In the hilltowns, the terrain and soil had been poorly suited to growing staples but could be adapted to dairying and orchards.[2]

An enlarged market also allowed manufacturers to expand and to operate firms with many, sometimes several hundred, employees. But widened competition prompted a drive for efficiency, and only those producers with some special advantage in organization, location, or technology could long prosper. Specialization often resulted in places generating goods for which they were peculiarly suited. Thus, the five towns developed different production patterns depending on their natural advantages or lack of them.

Damaged by Jeffersonian policies and a changed international situation, Salem's shipping declined after 1815. However, some merchants continued in a coasting trade which provided access to raw materials and to markets for finished products. This trade gave Salem economic advantages which eventually produced widespread manufacturing. But all the pieces had to fit together first. Until the late 1830s, Salem's economy remained tied to a carrying trade which did not involve finishing goods except for copal, rubber, and leather. Local tanneries boomed as merchants brought hides to be treated and sold as leather to Essex County boot and shoe manufacturers. But, since it was not easily subject to technological innovation, tanning remained small-scale, with 25 or so men employed in each works. Expansion took place incrementally through establishment of new firms.

Rapid, sustained growth came only in the 1840s with the expansion of Salem's coasting trade in coal. Coupled with the steam engine and readily available raw materials such as cotton, this source of cheap power gave Salem unique advantages and allowed her to develop large-scale manufacturing. The Naumkeag Steam Cotton Mills, reputed to be one of the largest and most efficient factories in the country, were completed in 1848. As the Naumkeag idea spread, coal and steam power drove Salem toward rapid economic development.

Depending on a seaborne trade which brought raw materials and coal, Salem's economic recovery in the 1850s developed out of mercantile activity. Two patterns could be found. First, Salem acted as a supplier of materials (e.g., coal, leather) necessary for manufacturing in interior towns. Second, Salem became a manufacturing center to which goods such as cotton were brought to be finished and then shipped down the coast or abroad. In this second pattern, manufacturing was the intermediate phase in a three-part process dominated throughout by merchants. Despite the decline of Salem's commerce, her economy remained tied to the sea; this discouraged diversity and led to concentration on coal, cotton, and leather.

Worcester depended on internal improvements for her development, and with the completion of the Blackstone Canal in 1829 and several railroads in the 1830s and 1840s, she began rapid, sustained progress toward the important manufacturing city which she had become by 1860. Unlike Salem, Worcester developed highly diverse manufacturing (boots and shoes, metal, machinery, wire, tools, agricultural implements, textiles, railroad equipment), none of which was part of a complex mercantile network as were the Naumkeag Mills. Worcester's many middle-sized establishments prospered in a situation where growth begat growth as profits were plowed back to generate new ventures. Because it provided extensive opportunity, Worcester's location encouraged capital to remain in town and spawned a wide variety of manufacturing endeavors.

With only a defunct canal and a north-south railroad completed in 1845, Northampton was not a prime site for manufacturing. Churning down from the hills to the west, the Mill River was harnessed to drive machinery. One large and several midsized manufacturing ventures grew up along its banks. However, no full-scale steam-driven operations appeared before 1860, and the Mill River neither descended rapidly nor did it possess a large volume of water. Restricted to an inadequate source of power, manufacturing establishments in Northampton were limited in scale and variety and were often enlargements of former artisan undertakings. Thirty miles to the south, the junction city of Springfield boomed, but without an east-west railroad Northampton did not.

Lacking transportation, Pelham and Ware had little chance to develop. Pelham languished without manufacturing or commerce, but Ware's excellent waterpower awaited exploitation by someone with capital and business experience. No local resident had such qualifications, but a group of Boston capitalists constructed three large textile factories in Ware in the late 1820s despite the town's otherwise disadvantageous location. Once built, these highly capitalized mills represented Ware's only economic development before 1860. Little local spinoff occurred as profits were siphoned off to Boston, so Ware remained a small factory village isolated in a rural backwater.

In both manufacturing and commerce, transportation and location in a hierarchy of cities appear to have been critical in influencing the course of economic development in the five towns. Relationships between hierarchical location and commerce seem clear, but some further discussion of manufacturing and overall economic development is in order. Let us review the sorts of economic contexts created in each of the five towns. Pelham's economy did not develop at all except for some increased commercial farming. Ware expanded suddenly in the late 1820s through the intrusion of outside capital. Employing almost all the town's work force, Ware's three large mills shut down periodically, changed owners several times, and did not stimulate other areas of the local economy except for dairying and market gardening. Without commerce and lacking diversity, Ware offered employment only on farms and in the mills, and opportunities in the mills fluctuated with the national market for textiles. After quick expansion, Ware stagnated, her economy following an erratic course.

Northampton grew steadily but slowly. Commerce, manufacturing, and agriculture all prospered, but none offered the sort of dynamism which could have triggered an extensive economic takeoff. Not highly capitalized, the town's many small manufacturing firms did not stimulate expansion. There was no large local spinoff or multiplier effect. Lacking excellent transportation and sources of power and threatened by Springfield's emergence as a junction city, Northampton's diverse, slowly expanding economy offered continuing but limited opportunities for economic gain. However, after 1855, Northampton did obtain a north-south railroad which bypassed Springfield, and the town also became the site of a large state hospital and several water-cure health establishments. Between 1855 and 1860 Northampton's population grew rapidly, but growth came more from the hospital and health establishments than from manufacturing. Extensive economic expansion came only after 1860.

After the mid-1830s, all areas of Worcester's economy boomed. Commerce benefited from Worcester's important role as a junction city, agriculture prospered in response to population growth, and manufacturing began 40 years of relatively continuous and rapid expansion. Producing an extraordinary variety of goods, Worcester manufacturing firms ranged from small to large in capitalization,

TABLE 3.1
Population Changes, 1800–1860

	1800	1810	1820	1
Northampton	2,190	2,631	2,854	3,
Worcester	2,411	2,577	2,962	4,
Ware	997	996	1,154	2,
Salem	9,457	12,613	12,731	13,
Pelham	1,144	1,185	1,278	

NOTE: A description of all tables may be found in the appendix.
* Pelham lost territory between 1820 and 1830. Her population appe. have remained stable during these ten years.

numbers of employees, and value of product. Still, no really large operations (500–600 employees) could be found in Worcester, and commercial and manufacturing profits generated readily available local capital. Metal working operations were common in Worcester and did not require much initial funding. Many of these firms with small investments sustained large returns which spun off into new activities. Growth of this sort, coupled with sharp increases in population, stimulated service and construction trades: stores, shops, and housebuilders prospered too. A diverse, wide-ranging, rapid expansion which fed on itself made Worcester a place of great promise.

Salem stagnated until the 1840s as her commerce declined but began to grow rapidly in the 1850s. Lacking Worcester's diversity, Salem depended primarily on leather, one large textile mill, and a carrying trade in coal and lumber. Vertically organized and dominated by merchants, Salem's economy remained tied to oceangoing trade. Profits and spinoff either went to merchants who could reinvest in any aspect of their operations or to tanners and curriers who lacked technological skills to generate development outside their own trade. As of 1860, spinoff seems not to have played an important local role—perhaps profits were reinvested outside town. In any case, growth had not yet begun to reproduce itself.

Demographic Changes

Improved transportation and the rise of manufacturing led to increased concentration of population, that is, to urbanization. Table 3.1 gives information on population increase. Two points merit emphasis here. First, population changes for the most part paralleled

1837	1840	1850	1855	1860
3,576	3,750	5,278	5,819	6,788
7,117	7,497	17,049	22,286	24,960
2,403	1,890	3,785	3,498	3,597
14,985	15,082	20,264	20,934	22,252
957	956	983	789	748

economic development, with decline in Pelham, slow, steady growth in Northampton until 1855, very rapid expansion in Worcester, erratic fluctuation in Ware, and relative stagnation in Salem until 1840, followed by expansion. Brought about by the state hospital and the water-cure establishments, Northampton's rapid growth between 1855 and 1860 was the only exception. Second, in 1860 Northampton, Ware, and Pelham remained small communities but Worcester and Salem did not. These differences in size meant that the larger two cities faced problems relating to sewage disposal, water supply, streets, police and fire protection, housing, schools, and care of the poor which either did not exist in the smaller places or were greatly reduced in scale. Sheer population size thus formed a critical element in defining social context which made Worcester and Salem very different from the other three towns.

Most population growth came through in-migration. Until the mid-1840s in-migrants were predominantly young men and women from New England. In developing towns, the ranks of unattached young adults swelled until in 1850 people aged 16 to 30 formed more than one-third of the population in all towns but Pelham. Roughly one person in seven was aged 16 to 30, single, and not living with his or her parents.

After about 1845 these young New Englanders were joined by Irish and other immigrants who in the following ten years became about one-quarter of the population of all of our towns but Pelham (table 3.2). Though the percentage of immigrants did not differ much from town to town, absolute numbers did. Large foreign populations could be found in Worcester (5,537) and Salem (4,398). Overall, foreigners and native young adults formed about one-half of the population in each of the developed towns.

TABLE 3.2

Foreign-Born Population in 1855

	Total population	% Foreign	N Foreign (includes unknown)	% Irish	N Irish
Northampton	5,819	24	1,383	16	918
Worcester	22,286	25	5,537	19	4,340
Ware	3,498	27	944	22	780
Salem	20,934	21	4,398	17	3,590
Pelham	789	02	13	01	7

Population increases were not spread evenly throughout the towns' territories. Some regions were left largely unaffected, at least in a physical sense, while others were totally transformed in a few years. In Northampton and Ware, new villages arose around the better water privileges. Similar growth took place in southern and eastern Worcester near the railroads, and in north Salem. Ware's development was probably the most striking. Between 1820 and 1828, a densely settled village of about 1,400 persons developed around new factories in the far southeastern corner of town, well away from the community's old center.[3]

Urbanization and manufacturing also led to the growth of new semiautonomous communities or villages which were dedicated to a few economic activities or even to a single one. Residents of the manufacturing villages, mostly laborers, lived within a short walk of their work. Nearby stores provided for their basic needs so that there would have been little reason for them to cross over into another part of town. Each of the developing towns produced these subcommunities; each subcommunity appears to have established some autonomy for itself.

All of the manufacturing villages arose on the edge of older town centers. Partly this pattern derived from availability of cheap land, but more important was the desire of entrepreneurs to locate near sources of power and/or transportation. In Northampton and Ware, sites outside old centers offered sources of waterpower. Factory owners located there and villages developed around the new operations. In Ware, such growth overwhelmed the former center, but Northampton's factory villages remained subservient to the older commercial-legal center partly because the new villages were small and partly because some of them were located outside town limits.

Location of areas for expansion in Worcester and Salem resulted primarily from the availability of transportation facilities. But power and transportation cannot be divorced, for larger industries in both towns depended on steam power derived from imported coal. Worcester's early industrial development took place along the Blackstone Canal and River and the Mill Brook, an area which afforded both power and transportation. This area long remained a manufacturing center but was gradually replaced as railroads opened new regions in south and east Worcester. As construction of spur lines was completed, new operations quickly occupied formerly vacant areas along them.

Salem's manufacturing centers arose, like Worcester's, near railroad lines, but their location was probably more dependent on wharf-

age facilities, especially the Naumkeag and Phillips wharves. Both
wharves eased problems of bringing in coal from Pennsylvania and
improved the town's capacity to import lumber, hides, and cotton, as
well as to export finished products. Without these facilities, Salem's
large steam planing and cotton mills could not have operated profitably.

Located along the river in the northern and western part of town,
Salem's leather industries had long occupied this part of the city,
which was so convenient for unloading and processing hides and
tanbark. The Essex Railroad which ran along the river did not, then,
cause persons in the leather trades to pick this location, but it did
encourage expansion in this area.

Dedicated as they were to manufacturing, these subcommunities
were primarily peopled by various types of laborers and artisans,
along with a few overseers, clerks, resident agents, and owners.
Usually, too, a few greengrocers and a variety store or two were to be
found, along with saloons in the larger towns of Worcester and
Salem. Property ownership tended to be less common in these areas
than in the community at large and the property less valuable. For
example, in 1850, in Worcester's fifth ward (a manufacturing area)
74% of the males aged 16 and over were workingmen, and about 50%
of those adult males listed were foreign born. In this area, ownership
of real estate was about one-half as common (16% as compared to
32.5%) as in some other parts of Worcester.[4]

In older parts of town, similar walking communities existed, but
they were dedicated to other (i.e., nonmanufacturing) purposes. The
Essex-Church-Front-Washington Street area of Salem, the Main-
Exchange-Market-Union Street part of Worcester, and the Main
Street portion of Northampton all functioned as centers of exchange.
Here were located the banks, insurance companies, large merchants
and storekeepers, along with numerous services, merchant tailors,
shoemakers, and the like. Here, too, could be found hotels, the market, boardinghouses, the town hall, and county courthouse.

By 1860, these commercial centers were more crowded than they
had been and were more involved with transportation and the needs
of manufacturing. The volume of business sharply increased, but the
character of the activities carried on in the old centers (legal, financial,
commercial) had not changed a great deal from earlier times. Merchants, bankers, and lawyers lived near these business centers—usually within three or four blocks. Salem's wealthy congregated near the
business center along Chestnut and Essex streets and around Wash-
ington Square; most of Northampton's were along Main Street and

on the Round Hill; while Worcester's could be found in the Elm Street area.

Other neighborhoods are harder to identify and appear to have been small clusters of homes or tenements rather than large units. Main streets were often filled with native artisans while the alleys were mostly Irish. A boardinghouse in an all-Irish area of Worcester was all-Yankee. Yankee and Irish poor tended to be intermixed along Salem's waterfront. The very richest neighborhood in Worcester was but a short walk from the poorest Irish-labor area of the city. These pocket neighborhoods can be found in the new subcommunities at the periphery as well as in old central parts of the towns, and seem to have been a common phenomenon of antebellum cities.

The tendency of urban growth to give rise to peripherally located subcommunities had a centrifugal effect on the internal structure of Worcester and Salem. Residents were dispersed outward, away from old population centers. Where formerly there had been one relatively small, commercially focused, walking community and an agricultural hinterland, by 1860 there stood several interdependent but geographically separated and partly autonomous communities, each with fairly specialized economic interests and a limited selection of persons in various occupations and economic strata. The agricultural hinterland remained. Because they were much smaller, Ware and Northampton did not develop this decentralized subcommunal pattern but rather produced distinctly separate factory villages located near waterpower.

Relatively small factory villages of the sort that developed in Ware and Northampton lent themselves to social and economic control by manufacturers and to limited economic opportunities for workingmen. Manufacturers could keep an eye on their employees and, as owners of stores, factories, and housing, they held enormous discretionary authority. Workingmen had little chance to rise occupationally in this sort of situation.

Subcommunal development in the larger places of Worcester and Salem did not lend itself to informal social control, as employees of many firms mixed in together and company housing and stores were not to be found. In this arrangement, workingmen had much greater chances to become storekeepers and boardinghouse owners, and social controls could only come from more formal institutionalized sources. Population dispersion and subcommunities of workingmen would also have a political impact when a system of ward elections was introduced.

◄§ 4 §►

Geographic Mobility

RECENT RESEARCH ON GEOGRAPHIC mobility in America's antebellum period has found an extraordinary amount of movement, so much movement that some historians have wondered how any social order could have been maintained. In our study of the five towns, then, we must first find out just how much mobility took place and then determine whether or not it provoked personal alienation and social disorder.[1]

Levels of Movement

Was there a high level of geographic mobility between 1850 and 1860? Yes there was, and levels of movement in the five towns seem consistent with those which scholars such as Peter Knights have established for other communities. About two-thirds of the male residents aged 16 and over who appear in the five Massachusetts towns' 1850 censuses do not reappear ten years later. Table 4.1 shows rates of persistence for the five towns, but data for Salem are from the 1850 census and an 1859 city directory. No correction has been made for deaths.

In the light of the communities' differing economic structures and their varying levels of population increase, the general similarity of rates of adult-male loss is striking. Static Pelham, for example, shows a pace of exodus about the same as that of dynamic Worcester. The similarity of these figures suggests that the impetus behind out-migration was not simply urbanization or economic change but a more generalized impulse which affected agricultural, nonurban places as well.

However, rates of exodus from the towns were probably not as similar as they at first seem. Both Ware and Northampton had a higher percentage of employed females than did Worcester or Salem.

If these young women moved as often as their male counterparts, then out-migration rates would increase relatively more in the two former towns. The very large number of females in Ware's textile mills would have pushed rates of removal there substantially higher than in any of the other communities. With these corrections, removal would range from high to low from Ware to Northampton-Worcester-Salem to Pelham.

Removal alone gives an incomplete picture of mobility, for many newcomers moved into town while others were leaving. Using the rates of persistence shown in table 4.1, we can calculate the number of out-migrants and newcomers. Added together, out-migrants and newcomers give the *minimum* number of people who moved in or out of each town between 1850 and 1860. Summarized in table 4.2, this procedure is somewhat suspect because it assumes that the whole population moved at a pace comparable to that of adult males. Still, despite this flaw, minimum population turnover does give us a more complete view of overall movement.[2]

Mobility was indeed high: 9,110 people moved in or out of Northampton; 30,415 in or out of Worcester; more than 5,000 moved in or out of Ware; and about 27,000 either entered or left Salem. The extent of such movement appears similar to, but somewhat less than, that which Peter Knights found in Boston. Knights concluded that at least twice as many households passed through Boston as lived in the city during a single decade.

Though it was generally high in all communities but Pelham, minimum population turnover varied among the towns in both the size and the relative influence of in- and out-migration. Out-migration

TABLE 4.1
Persistence, 1850–1860, of Males Aged 16 and Over in 1850

	N	% Reappearing (persisters)	% Removed or died
Northampton	1,109	28	72
Worcester*	1,263	34	66
Ware	946	29	71
Salem†	1,356	38	62
Pelham	216	36	64

* Data for Worcester and Salem are based on 25% samples.
† Data for Salem from 1850 census and 1859 city directory.

played a greater proportional role in turnover in Ware, and in-migration had more impact in Salem, Northampton, and Worcester. For example, Ware's turnover ratio of 1.37 was produced by .71 out-migration and .66 newcomers, but Worcester's 1.78 ratio came from .66 out-migration and 1.12 newcomers.

Whatever its internal components, minimum turnover ratios were much higher in Worcester and Northampton than in Ware and Salem. Why should this be so? Why should more people move in and out of the two former towns? The answer appears to lie in a combined influence of economic expansion and location in an urban hierarchy. Expansion provided opportunities which attracted newcomers. As focal points of transportation within an established hinterland, middle- and upper-level sites underwent greater population turnover. Moving along established routes, people naturally flowed in and out of Worcester and, to a lesser extent, Northampton. But such movement would not take someone through either Salem or Ware.

Even the apparently high rates of minimum population turnover severely underestimate mobility for they do not include people who moved in and out without appearing on census rolls. City directories allow us to correct this defect in our data but, since directories are unavailable for towns other than Worcester and Salem, we can only calculate maximum population turnover for those two places.[3]

Twenty-eight percent of the males listed in the 1850 Worcester city directory do not reappear in 1851. Absence could reflect death, migration, or error on the part of the publisher but, if we project the 28% rate to the population as a whole, about 4,500 people would have moved out in this one year. Yet Worcester's population grew on the

TABLE 4.2
Minimum Population Turnover, 1850–1860

	Population in 1850	N Out-migrants	N New-comers	Total N movers	Total movers ÷ 1850 population
Northampton	5,278	3,800	5,310	9,110	1.73
Worcester	17,049	11,252	19,163	30,415	1.78
Ware	3,785	2,687	2,499	5,186	1.37
Salem	20,264	12,564	14,552	27,116	1.34
Pelham	983	629	394	1,023	1.04

average of about 500 people per year, so some 5,000 people must have entered town. Such calculations are very rough, but they indicate that as many as 100,000 persons may have entered and left Worcester in the 1850s. Salem's figures are not nearly as impressive, though her 17% annual out-migration suggests a maximum turnover of 65,000 or 70,000 during 1850–1860. Why the differences between Salem and Worcester? We cannot be very sure, but they were probably due to variations in hierarchical location and the flow-through process encouraged by Worcester's excellent transportation.

People also moved within the two towns: 23% annually in Worcester and 18% in Salem. If these persons are added to in- and out-migrants, then the total number of movers during the decade approaches 150,000 in Worcester and 100,000 in Salem. Was there a high rate of geographic mobility? Yes. Astounding rates of movement could be found which appear to have varied in terms of locus in a hierarchy of cities and the pace of economic expansion.

Increase in Geographic Mobility

Did geographic mobility increase between 1800 and 1860? Yes, but our data will not allow us to be very sure of the size of increases, though they do not appear as great as might have been expected. Since the 1800 federal census lists only heads of households, we must compare the relative propensity for out-migration among such per-

---

TABLE 4.3
Removal of Native-Born Heads of Households, 1800–1810, 1850–1860

	N	% Removed or died (1850–1860)	N	% Removed or died (1800–1810)	Change in 1850–1860 over 1800–1810 (% points)
Northampton	539	59	380	48	+11
Worcester*	832	57	369	48	+ 9
Ware	616	68	135	44	+24
Salem*	908	61	1,572	48	+13
Pelham	162	59	147	61	− 2

* Data for Worcester and Salem are based on 25% samples.

sons for the two periods 1800–1810 and 1850–1860. Only native Americans are included in table 4.3, to assure that any increases are not a result of the entry of highly mobile foreigners in the later period.

The surprisingly high levels of out-migration for 1800–1810 indicate that substantial movement preceded economic development and innovations in transportation. In most towns about one-half the heads of households moved out (or died) between 1800 and 1810 and, except for Ware, increases in mobility over the next half century were only about ten percentage points—rather less than might have been expected. Nevertheless, actual increases may have been larger than these figures suggest. In all towns but Pelham, heads of households formed a larger part of the population in 1800 than they did in 1850. Single persons appear to have represented an increased proportion of the population in the later period. Assuming that the relative tendency of heads and singles to move remained equal in both periods, the overall rate of out-migration of a town's population would have increased even if movement among heads had remained constant, because a higher percentage of town population in 1850 was made up of more mobile young and single people. If singles, like heads, showed a greater proclivity to move in 1850, then overall rates of mobility must have increased substantially.

Using the 1800–1810 removal percentages from table 4.3, we can calculate minimum population turnover (see table 4.4). Turnover appears much lower than it was in 1850–1860. However, it must be remembered that our calculations are based on heads of households

TABLE 4.4

Minimum Population Turnover, 1800–1810

	Population in 1800	N *Out-migrants*	N *New-comers*	*Total* N *movers*	*Total movers ÷ 1800 population*
Northampton	2,190	1,051	1,492	2,543	1.16
Worcester	2,411	1,157	1,323	2,480	1.03
Ware	997	439	438	877	0.88
Salem	9,457	4,539	7,695	12,234	1.29
Pelham	1,144	698	739	1,437	1.26

and underestimate mobility among the whole population. Nevertheless, a minimum of 12,000 people moved through Salem, about 2,500 through Worcester and Northampton, 1,400 entered or left Pelham, and almost 900 moved in Ware. Such figures belie the image of sleepy New England towns which basked in stability. Mobility increased during the first one-half of the nineteenth century, yet it was not a new process and existed at high levels before widespread urbanization or economic development had taken place.

Even if rates of population turnover did not rise as much as might have been expected, the scale certainly did. The sheer number of movers rose strikingly between 1800 and 1860. In 1800, when these movers were deemed a social problem, they were simply chased out of town—warned out, as it were. In 1791, Salem selectmen warned out 261 residents who together with their families probably represented about 1,300 people or roughly 15% of the total population. While these figures are larger than most, the process itself was common throughout New England and seemed a convenient way to get rid of unwanted outsiders. But warning out could hardly cope with the 10,000 or so people who annually moved in Worcester in the 1850s. The scale of mobility had become too great for traditional techniques of control.

Nevertheless, if we assume, as some historians have, that the process of mobility in itself alienated individuals and disrupted communal solidarity, then we must recognize widespread movement in the very first decade of the nineteenth century before any of the symptoms associated with excessive mobility had appeared.

TABLE 4.5
Age and Removal, 1850–1860 (% removed or died in each age group)

	N	Age as of 1850					
		16–20	21–25	26–30	31–40	41–50	51–
Northampton	1,109	93.0	91	77	69	64	56
Worcester*	1,263	87.5	80	70	62	44	49
Ware	946	95.0	85	79	69	49	63
Salem*	1,356	76.0	75	64	61	51	42
Pelham	216	92.0	77	65	62	47	62

* Data for Worcester and Salem are based on 25% samples.

Who Moved and Who Stayed?

As shown in table 4.5, out-migration was higher among young members of the population. Moving with greater frequency than their elders, almost 90% of the young men left every town but Salem. In all towns, the rate of mobility dropped consistently as age increased up to 50 years. Over age 50 the rate of movement often rose again; this probably reflected a higher death rate in this sector of the populace.

Out-migrants were also more likely to engage in lower-status occupations. Table 4.6 shows relationships between occupation and out-migration. Persons in higher-status jobs—work which offered greater income and security—showed a lesser tendency to move out. Farmers, merchants, and professionals stayed much more frequently than did semi- and unskilled laborers. The rate of removal and death among unskilled laborers was consistently over 80%.

This connection between opportunity, security, and geographic mobility persists in relationships between movement and property holding. Table 4.7 shows the percentage of removal and death in each decile of real property. (Deciles were formed by taking all males over age 16, ranking them from richest to poorest, and then dividing them into ten equal parts. Thus, decile 1 represents the richest 10% of the adult males and decile 10 the poorest.) Again, basic relationships are consistent from town to town. Upper decile mobility is at a lesser rate

TABLE 4.6

Occupation and Out-Migration, 1850–1860
(% removed or died in each occupation group)

		Occupational Classification as of 1850			
	N	Farm	Merchant	Profes-sional	Manufactur
Northampton	1,109	36	43	59	63
Worcester*	1,263	41	40	38	47
Ware	946	52	37.5	75	80
Salem*	1,356	—	26	46	43
Pelham	216	63	50	50	—

* Data for Worcester and Salem are based on 25% samples, and thus the num in some cells may be based on only a few cases and may not be statisti significant.

than lower. It would appear that the more property a person owned the less he was inclined to move. In all towns, a sharp difference can be found between mobility among propertied and unpropertied persons. Note, for example, the break between the fourth and fifth deciles in Salem, the second and third in Worcester, the third and fourth in Northampton and Ware, and seventh and eighth deciles in Pelham.

Closer examination of property and mobility suggests that ownership itself rather than the amount owned was the critical factor. Table 4.8 presents data on removal among the propertied sector of the population. If the amount of property owned was of key influence, then removal should increase steadily from the first to the tenth decile. Some tendency in this direction may be noted, but it is not especially strong.

While young, unskilled, and poor people moved with remarkable frequency, other persons remained to provide a core of stability. Representing one-quarter or so of the towns' populations, these older, skilled, and propertied persisters sank roots and stayed many years, sometimes generations, while the overall population rapidly turned over every year. One hundred thousand people may have passed through Worcester in the 1850s, but 22% of her 1860 population had been there ten years before; 65,000 people apparently moved in and out of Salem between 1850 and 1860, yet 32% of her 1860 population

Business	White collar	Artisan, skilled	Semi-skilled	Labor	Ship captain	Sailor
67	84	74.5	81	95	—	—
61	63	59	83	82	—	—
75	75	70	87	86	—	—
45	61	53	64	89	21	77
67	100	70	—	85	—	—

was present in 1850. Persisters from 1850 formed 22% of Northampton's 1860 population, 31% in Ware, and 47% in Pelham.*

Most members of this stable sector of persisters were well-to-do persons who engaged in higher-status occupations which offered security and opportunity, but family also exerted a strong influence. The core families which had populated the towns in 1800 were still represented in 1860. Many members of these families had left, but they moved about one-half as often as the whole population and enough of them stayed behind to perpetuate blood ties with a century-old local past. Members of these old families joined with successful in-migrants and formed the base of the stable population.

A lifelong Worcester resident, Levi Lincoln, Jr., studied law with his father and went on to a distinguished career as an attorney and politician. Nine times governor of Massachusetts, speaker of the United States House of Representatives, first mayor of Worcester, Lincoln still found time to join in local affairs. An active member of the Unitarian Church, Lincoln presided over the Worcester County Agricultural Society, served as a director of the Worcester Bank, and participated in the American Antiquarian Society.

Lincoln's father had come to Worcester in 1775 where he led a remarkable life as an attorney and politician. After serving as lieutenant governor of Massachusetts, Lincoln, Sr., was appointed attorney general of the United States and associate justice of the United

---

* There are apparent inconsistencies between data presented here, in table 4.1, and table 7.2 (see p. 72). Probably the small sample used to calculate figures in table 7.2 accounts for discrepancies. Table 7.2 appears to exaggerate priority or persistence.

TABLE 4.7

Out-Migration and Wealth (% removed or died by decile)

		Richest				Wealth Decile, 1850					Poorest
	N	(1)	(2)	(3)	(4)	(5)	(6)	(7)	(8)	(9)	(10)
Northampton	1,109	47	56	54	74	85	85	85	85	85	85
Worcester*	1,263	38	53	77	77	77	77	77	77	77	77
Ware	946	41	53	65	82	82	82	82	82	82	82
Salem*	1,356	38	46	47	42	70	70	70	70	70	70
Pelham	216	33	50	50	69	63	65	60	85	85	85

* Data for Worcester and Salem are based on 25% samples.

States Supreme Court. Lincoln's mother was a Waldo (one of Worcester's wealthiest families), and his maternal grandmother was a Salisbury (one of the richest families in Massachusetts). Lincoln married into Worcester's leading eighteenth-century family—the Chandlers.

Influential in his own right, Lincoln had kin ties with the community's most powerful families, but he could also draw upon the strength of his immediate relatives. His two uncles lived in Worcester. John Lincoln served in several local political offices and voluntary associations while prospering in his mercantile business. William, the other uncle, wrote the first comprehensive history of Worcester, published the *Worcester Magazine*, served as a bank director, and edited a local newspaper. Lincoln's son, Daniel Waldo Lincoln, became a noted attorney. He was elected mayor, alderman, and representative to the Massachusetts General Court. He held directorships in several local banks, was director of the Boston and Worcester Railroad, and later became president of the Boston and Albany Railroad. Lincoln's grandchildren and great-grandchildren remained in Worcester where they followed distinguished careers as lawyers, doctors, and businessmen.

Here, then, was the basis for stability—long-resident people and families. Members of the Lincoln family lived in Worcester from 1775 until well into the twentieth century. Some members continue to live there today—200 years later. Successful and active in civic affairs, the Lincolns and their kin—the Salisburys, Waldos, Chandlers, and others—built institutions and sustained traditions which maintained continuity with the past.[4]

TABLE 4.8

Removal among Propertied Population (% removed or died by decile)

		Richest								Poorest	
	N	(1)	(2)	(3)	(4)	(5)	(6)	(7)	(8)	(9)	(10)
Northampton	287	43	39	58	60	49	55	61	50	68	68
Worcester*	201	33	45	45	50	54	42	42	47	60	57
Ware	325	27	55	55	46	46	52	42	60	53	64
Salem*	290	43	29	52	45	50	41	48	46	41	41
Pelham	153	39	57	57	48	48	67	69	75	65	65

Wealth Decile, 1850

* Data for Worcester and Salem are based on 25% samples.

Recognition of this stable population forces reconsideration of the nature of geographic mobility. Some people did not move, so each town had *two populations:* one stable and the other transient. Members of the stable sector remained for long periods while transients moved with extraordinary rapidity. Living near one another, owners of substantial homes and prosperous businesses, members of the stable sector were highly visible. Such visibility coupled with political and economic power allows us to see this stable group as *the* community. In many respects, such a view is correct. Members of the stable sector provided the continuity and cohesion that held society together. They ran the towns, held the political offices, supported the churches, and owned the stores and factories. They made the history of each town and they wrote it down. Yet, however visible, articulate, and powerful, this stable group formed a minority which confronted a highly transient majority two to three times its size.[5]

Why Did People Move?

Mobility of the sort we have found unquestionably provoked social problems which were at least new in scale if not in substance. We will return to this theme, but for the moment let us see if we can learn more about mobility and individuals.

Most of our data suggest that people moved because they had to—because they were pushed out by insecure employment. Unable to find sustained work, about 80% of the unskilled laborers left each town. In Northampton virtually all the factory operatives departed, and in Worcester roughly 90% of the boot and shoemakers moved out, so work in large, mechanized factories was apparently uncertain enough to prompt out-migration. But men employed in expanding and less mechanized trades were not as likely to leave. About one-third of Worcester's machinists, masons, and carpenters remained, as did one-third of Northampton's masons and 40% of her carpenters. Regardless of occupation, people with some limited resources could perhaps resist short-term unemployment, but unpropertied people had to find work quickly and so moved out almost as often as unskilled workers—about three-quarters of the unpropertied departed the towns between 1850 and 1860.

Data on wealth and occupation imply, then, that people were buffeted about in search of work. Pushed from here to there, alienated victims of an impersonal economic order, the unskilled and propertyless slipped into transiency. No doubt such a view contains substantial truth and possibly many, or even most, migrants were driven helplessly from place to place, but the correlation between age and mobility suggests that some qualifications may be in order.

About one-half the loss from the five towns involved young men under age 30. High mobility among the young, coupled with their proclivity to enter developing towns in large numbers, may help explain the extraordinary rates of movement that we have found. Young, mobile people went to the cities, so cities show high levels of mobility. Let us suppose that young men expected to move frequently during the early part of their lives. Socialized to achievement, they were expected (and themselves expected) to seek out opportunity and their place in the world. Free of wives and children, they could strive for success, security, and vertical mobility. They assumed that during this phase of their life they would have to move frequently, especially when prospects for local advancement seemed small. They chose, then, to move from place to place according to a coherent sense of how their lives were to develop. Departure from home and frequent moves induced stress, but this was assumed to be a temporary problem undergone for long-term gain.[6]

During this mobile phase of their lives, young men expected to concentrate their efforts on attaining security and a place for themselves to the exclusion of other concerns and involvements. The process of finding a place might take several years, and for some the dream of place and advancement was undoubtedly never fulfilled, but the dream was nevertheless there through these troubled years. Disillusionment would come later, if at all. In any event, young transients assumed that wandering was purposeful and would end. Then they could settle in, get married, have children, work hard, and buy property. They could shift their concerns. At this point, young men sought to expand their involvements, to participate in the community, and to move less often.

Study of the lives of successful men in Worcester County suggests that this hypothetical life cycle often existed in fact. Born between 1800 and 1840, about 20% of the 256 men whose complete biographies appear in Charles Nutt's *History of Worcester* (County) did not move during their adult lives. However, the remaining 80% averaged more than three intercommunal changes of residence. Most (70%) of these moves were made between the ages of 16 and 30, and more than one-half the men did not move after they were 30 years old. Only about one man in ten made more moves after age 30 than before.[7]

Such data indicate that our hypothetical life cycle bears some similarity to the lives of successful men who moved often in their youth but tended to slow down and settle in as they matured. The quality of movement also fits our life cycle though the evidence is highly impressionistic. Youthful moves commonly involved acquisition of skills (e.g., an apprenticeship) or employment in a relative's store or shop. Shifts in residence at a later age seem to have been designed to improve economic opportunities (e.g., moves to communities with better transportation and/or sources of power). Movement appeared purposeful and rational rather than random, though many moves proved to be failures. These successful Worcesterites may have moved frequently but they were not transients.

Of course, our data base excludes transients whose biographies would not appear in a county history. But nothing especially distinguishes those men who do appear except that in the long run they attained some local eminence. That is, their early backgrounds were diverse and relatively similar to the New England population at large, so one might suppose that at least their youthful patterns of movement resembled those of less successful men. Differences would be more likely to appear after age 30 with the less successful more inclined to continue to move. In any case, mobility among successful men appears to have been sensibly patterned around acquisition of skills and pursuit of economic advantage. Among successful men mobility was less a source of alienation than a stimulus to personal advancement. Successful men moved in order to improve their life chances.

Even if many men did not adhere to this mobility pattern, examples of highly mobile and successful men were always before them. One of Worcester's richest and most distinguished citizens, Ichabod Washburn, moved nine times before he was 21 years old. As a penniless young man, Washburn went from place to place learning about metal working and machinery until he arrived in Worcester in 1819, settled in, and established himself as a wire manufacturer. Active in public affairs—especially education for mechanics and artisans—Washburn and his career were widely known, and if on the one hand he was a classic case of a poor boy who made good, Washburn also showed that geographic mobility could pay off. Numerous other successful migrants reaffirmed Washburn's example, so the career models before Worcester's young men frequently linked success and mobility.[8]

Why did people move? We cannot be sure. Many moved because they had been pushed out and needed to find employment. No doubt some of the least skilled became floaters or permanent transients. But others appear to have migrated rationally, acquiring skills and moving among relatives and friends to more advantageous sites so as to improve themselves. All men could look toward examples of the many successful people who prospered through mobility, and young men probably assumed that their ambitions would only be fulfilled through frequent movement. As an expected part of one's life cycle, mobility would not have prompted widespread alienation except perhaps when it continued into middle age.

Mobility and Social Stability

Was mobility excessive enough to overwhelm the social order and usher in an age of relative chaos? The question is value laden and ambiguous. What, after all, do the words *excessive, overwhelm, social order,* and *chaos* mean? Yet, for all its uncertainties, the question has played an important if latent role in recent historical research and deserves an answer. Let us look first at the effect of mobility on individuals and then at its impact on communities.

Individual responses to mobility probably varied with the ability to integrate movement into a cohesive view of self and relationships between self and others. *Order* and *chaos* here represent states of mind in which mobility does or does not make sense in relation to one's larger expectations about himself and his life. Mobility thus becomes excessive when it threatens to make nonsense of someone's life by destroying coherence and purpose.

By these standards, how excessive was mobility for residents of the five Massachusetts towns? Members of the stable population did not move, and so between 20% and 47% of the towns' people remained unaffected by mobility. About one-third of the townsmen left as young men under age 30 who probably had coherent life-cycle explanations for movement. Another 10% to 15% migrated as skilled *and* propertied men over age 30, most of whom may be assumed to have planned moves to places offering greater economic opportunities.

Taking the towns' 1850 adult male population as a whole then, about 25% did not move, 30% left as young men, and another 10% to 15% probably plotted moves for economic advancement. If this is correct, 60% to 70% of the adult males should not have suffered from "excessive" mobility. Movement among the remaining 30% or 40% may have threatened to bring incoherence but, stimulated by the examples of men like Ichabod Washburn, many of them may have clung to hopes and meanings drawn from life-cycle expectations yet to be fulfilled.

What of mobility and community? Even if most individuals could move and still sustain a sense of coherence, would not the sheer scale of mobility have disrupted communal solidarity? If community is defined in terms of participation in a network of relationships and institutions, mobility did not have much impact. Members of the stable population maintained public institutions and voluntary associations over long periods of time. These affiliations and involvements brought coherence and long-term stability to a community in which migrants seldom if ever joined. Stable and mobile people occupied the same geographic space, but they were two separate populations and the volatility of the mobile sector did not disrupt continuity in the stable one.

To be sure, the presence of many young, poor, and highly mobile people created problems for members of the stable sector and changed the context in which they lived. Confronted with numerous strangers, stable members had to develop new means of social control, such as the police. But, as we shall see later, innovations in control mechanisms tended to appear only in larger cities, opening the possibility that urbanization (i.e., large-scale concentration of population) encouraged experiments in social control more than did mobility.

To argue that mobility was not "excessive" is not to deny its significance. Mobility certainly affected family structure by lessening the influence of extrahousehold ties. It perplexed people by placing them in unfamiliar contexts and thus prompted the rise of new associations and behavior through which people sought to acclimatize themselves and recreate familiar and comforting elements of their former lives. And mobility selectively redistributed population westward and into the cities with ambitious men and women seeking out areas of greater opportunity.

We should also be sensitive to a larger issue here. Our hypothetical life cycle assumes that residents of the five towns and their contemporaries held a "liberal" or "atomistic" view of society. This view was based on the idea that individuals were the crucial social unit and assumed that as people separately pursued their private interests some larger public or social good would emerge. However, we argued earlier that New Englanders relied on traditions which held that patriarchal communities were the basis for a healthy social order. These two conceptions of society are not easily reconciled for they involve fundamentally different evaluations of proper social arrangements. Certainly the atomistic view was well suited to the rapidly changing, urbanized, and market-oriented society which New Englanders were busily creating, but patriarchal traditions were deeply entrenched and conflict between these differing conceptions of the social order prompted a "cultural crisis" of major proportions.

Somewhere in this cultural crisis and the social changes which surrounded it lies the basis for understanding the history of New England between 1830 and 1860. The crisis was complex in its own right and the linkages between it and social change were extraordinarily diverse, but the central dilemma for people at that time was to gain some means for grappling with problems of freedom and authority in an era of rapid change. Their efforts to do so led to that release of human creativity in religion, literature, and social criticism which we know as the New England Renaissance.

✌§ 5 ৡ✍

Wealth Distribution

MOST STUDIES OF URBAN wealth distribution have found highly unequal patterns of ownership, with the richest 10% of the population owning 75% of the property or even more. Such distributions have been taken as evidence of highly stratified and relatively closed societies. Our study of Massachusetts towns points to somewhat different conclusions and argues that wealth distribution must be seen in relation to age and economic activity. Let's look at our data and the questions raised in chapter 1.

How Was Wealth Distributed in 1860?

Except for Pelham, wealth in 1860 was owned in highly unequal shares. Table 5.1 shows the distributions for males aged 16 and over. In Salem, Ware, and Northampton, the richest 10% of the adult males owned about 70% of the real and personal wealth listed on the federal census schedules or local tax lists. In Worcester, the figure for the richest decile rises to almost 90% but falls to only 28% in Pelham. Striking as such figures are, they underestimate the degree of concentration. In Ware, Northampton, and Salem, the wealthiest 1% of the men held about 25% of the property, and in Worcester that group owned more than 40% of the town's wealth. These proportions appear reasonably typical of the nation at large where the richest 1% of the adult males held 30% of the real estate in 1850.[1]

Pelham's 4% ownership by the richest 1% is the only situation approaching parity, but then, no one should expect property to have been owned in absolutely equal shares in Pelham or anywhere else. American emphasis on achievement insured inequality for, even if everyone began at the same point, differential talents, skills, career choices, and luck would have promoted unequal ownership. The problem here is a serious one. At first sight, we may be tempted to deplore a society characterized by inequalities as large as those shown in table 5.1, but we had better reserve judgment for as yet we have no sure basis for knowing what our figures for wealth distribution mean.

Let's go back to the life-cycle model presented in the previous chapter and see if we can develop some basis for evaluating our data on wealth ownership. That life-cycle model suggested that men spent a period of youthful wandering and then settled in at about age 30 and began to accumulate property. We might, therefore, assume that all men aged 16 to 30 would not own property and that men aged 31 and over would have begun gradually to acquire an estate. No doubt the process of accumulation was uncertain and sporadic rather than steadily upward, but let's assume a regular and continuous growth in wealth from age 31 until death of $200 per year. Thus, men aged 16 to 30 would own no property, a 31-year-old would own $200, a 32-year-old $400, a 40-year-old $2,000, a 50-year-old $4,000, and so on. Such an assumption is highly artificial. Certainly no one followed the $200-per-year model suggested here. Still, the model should give us a better means for judging actual distributions and, despite the model's arbitrary nature, it fits reasonably well with Lee Soltow's findings on property holding in the United States between 1850 and 1870.[2]

Soltow examined a sample of adult males from the federal censuses, 1850–1870, and noted a strong tendency for men to become owners of real estate as they became older. Furthermore, these holdings steadily increased in value until age 45 or so. Soltow "suggests that wealth accumulation begins about age 18 and is directly proportional to adult age." He posits an annual accumulation rate of about 6%. Nevertheless, the younger men in Soltow's sample owned very small amounts of real estate, so our model seems relatively consistent with his findings.[3]

TABLE 5.1
Wealth Distribution in 1860 (% owned per decile)

		Richest								Poorest	
	N	(1)	(2)	(3)	(4)	(5)	(6)	(7)	(8)	(9)	(10)
Northampton	1,472	72	19.0	8	1.0	—	—	—	—	—	—
Worcester	4,241	87	11.0	2	0.5	—	—	—	—	—	—
Ware	1,283	71	18.0	7	2.0	1.5	0.5	—	—	—	—
Salem	4,632	69	17.0	8	4.0	2.0	—	—	—	—	—
Pelham	224	28	20.5	16	11.0	9.0	8.0	5	2	0.2	—

Table 5.2 presents distributions of wealth for four towns, based on the $200 model and the actual ages of adult males. (Illegibility of much of the 1860 Salem census prohibited her inclusion.)

Except for Pelham, the richest deciles owned between 35% and 44% of the wealth. About 40% of the male population was unpropertied, though Pelham again varies from the other towns. Pelham's distribution here looks rather like the actual one presented in table 5.1, but comparison of actual and model distributions (tables 5.1 and 5.2) in the other towns shows that the richest actual decile owned much more wealth than the model's and the ranks of the actually unpropertied were larger than the model predicts. Nevertheless, note that the model does not produce anything like equality in the developed towns.

Why do these differences appear between actual and model distributions? Can our model be revised to improve its accuracy? The model works well for men aged 16 to 40. Virtually everyone under age 30 did not own property, and more than one-half of those between 31 and 40 fell within the $200 to $2,000 range which the model suggests, or were very close to it. However, after age 41, more and more men begin to fall behind the model's predictions. Our initial correction, then, is to establish age 40 as a plateau beyond which accumulation slows or ceases altogether. The "normal" pattern now becomes one of no property, age 16 to 30; accumulation, age 31 to 40; and relative stability, age 41 and over.

Despite this correction, many men still do not fit. Of those persons aged 31 and over, 40% to 50% never acquired more than tiny amounts of property and may be designated *casualties*. William Harris, a 52-year-old teamster, lived in Northampton in 1850. Harris did

TABLE 5.2

Wealth Distribution Based on Actual Age and the $200 Model
(% of wealth owned per decile)

		Richest								Poorest	
	N	(1)	(2)	(3)	(4)	(5)	(6)	(7)	(8)	(9)	(10)
Northampton	1,472	38	24	17	11	7	3	—	—	—	—
Worcester	4,241	44	25	17	9	4	1	—	—	—	—
Ware	1,283	35	24	17	12	7	4	—	—	—	—
Salem*	—	—	—	—	—	—	—	—	—	—	—
Pelham	224	29	21	16	14	11	6	3	0.2	—	—

* Data unavailable for Salem.

not own any real estate. Ten years later, now in his sixties, Harris still made his home in Northampton but he had not been able to accumulate any real or personal property. All in their thirties in 1850, Isaac G. Damon (carpenter), Henry Noble (carriage maker), and Isaac P. Davis (blacksmith) struggled unsuccessfully for the next ten years. None of these three men owned any property in 1850 or 1860. Men like Davis, Damon, Noble, and Harris joined with many others in similarly difficult situations. Some of these propertyless or poor men stayed in town, some drifted from place to place, but all were apparent *casualties* of a social system which denied them property.

Living in the same towns with these casualties, wealthy men could be found whose property holdings exceeded our model's norms. John Fowle of Northampton owned $6,800 in real estate in 1850 when he was but 30 years old. By age 40, Fowle had accumulated $10,000 in real and personal property. Charles Delano, a 39-year-old attorney, already possessed an estate worth $66,000 in 1860. Henry Bright, aged 66, held property valued at $105,000 in 1860. County sheriff and judge Samuel Hinckley had amassed an estate listed at $155,000 in 1860. Hinckley was 49 years old.

Our model bears little relevance to men such as Hinckley, Delano, and Fowle, so we need to include an *elite* composed of rich men of all ages along with our casualties. We now have four groups: the youthful unpropertied and poor, the middle stratum of men over age 30 who fit the model's norms, the wealthy elite, and the unpropertied or poor casualties over age 30.

The presence of the casualties and the elite helps explain much of the discrepancy between actual wealth distributions shown in table 5.1 and the model distributions presented in table 5.2. The elite owned sharply disproportionate shares of wealth and the casualties possessed little or none. Both groups thus contributed to the high proportion of property held by the richest decile and to the gap between model and reality. If these two groups are removed from calculations, property distributions are about what the model would suggest, with the richest decile owning roughly 33% of the wealth.

The towns' highly unequal wealth distributions are not, then, a product of a highly stratified society composed primarily of rich and poor but must be seen in relation to age and the relative size of four groups of men: young, elite, middle stratum, and casualties. Our property distributions reflect a society devoted to achievement, in which the young generally did not own property, a few men prospered inordinately, many men over 30 failed to gain even minimal material success, but in which about one-half the men over 30 attained moderate holdings as members of the middle stratum. The relative size of these groups, especially the young, elite, and the casualties, controlled the dimensions of actual distributions, and, as we shall soon see, the size of the groups varied considerably from town to town. Nevertheless, highly unequal wealth distribution did not reflect simple affluence and poverty but grew out of a society with a substantial and prosperous middle stratum.

Wealth Distribution and Economic Activity

Property ownership was a function of economic activity, with commerce and manufacture encouraging unequal ownership and agriculture promoting greater parity. Common in upper-level, commercial areas such as Worcester, large retail and wholesale establishments with shops and inventories valued at several thousand dollars represented substantial accumulations of wealth not to be found in rural places. Manufacturing also generated sizable holdings sometimes valued at more than $100,000. Customarily sole proprietorships or partnerships, these large shops and manufacturing plants expanded the ranks of what we have designated the elite. That is, they created a situation in which a few men owned great amounts of property.

Shops and manufacturing establishments not only encouraged a few large holdings but also brought many employees into the area. These employees, who often lacked wealth, swelled the ranks of the young and casualties until three-quarters or more of the adult males owned little or no property (table 5.1). In 1860, two cotton mills in Ware employed 147 men, each of whom was paid a monthly wage of about $20. The owners of the mills, Charles Stevens and George Gilbert, were listed as owners of more than $200,000 worth of personal and real estate.[4]

On the other hand, agriculture in the five towns produced neither very large holdings nor numerous poor employees. About 70% of our farmers owned property, a proportion two or three times that of the general population. These figures appear reasonably typical of New England where, in 1850, 63% of the farmers owned real estate—roughly double the 32% real property owners among the whole population.[5]

Generally valued between $3,000 and $5,000, farms represented comfortable but not particularly large holdings. Most farmers did not employ help on a permanent basis, and those who did commonly used only a few men. Thus, the richest 10% of the farmers in the five towns owned only 30% to 40% of the agricultural wealth, while in the whole town the richest 10% held 75% or more of the property.

Variations in agricultural and nonagricultural distributions may be observed cross-sectionally at one time, as for example in the differences between Pelham and the other towns, or between agricultural and nonagricultural sectors of a single town's economy. They may also be seen historically as a community's economic emphasis shifted from farming to other ventures. Table 5.3 presents both historical and cross-sectional comparisons for Northampton. In 1800, the richest decile of the whole population owned 50% of the wealth, but the richest 10% of the farmers held only 34% of the agricultural property. As Northampton acquired more commerce and manufacturing, the upper decile's portion of the town's estate rose to 72% and the ranks of the unpropertied more than doubled to about 70%. However, agricultural distributions remained almost stable between 1800 and 1860.

This relationship between wealth distribution and economic activity remains true of areas outside Northampton and our other towns. For example, James Henretta has shown how property ownership became more centralized in eighteenth-century Boston as the town developed commercially, and Lee Soltow has demonstrated that, in

TABLE 5.3

Agricultural and Total Wealth Distribution, 1800 and 1860: Northampton (% owned per decile)

	N	Richest (1)	(2)	(3)	(4)	(5)	(6)	(7)	(8)	Poorest (9)	(10)
1800											
Whole population	483	50	18.5	12.5	8.5	6	3.5	1	—	—	—
Agriculture only	421	34	23.0	13.0	12.0	10	7.0	1	—	—	—
1860											
Whole population	1,472	72	19.0	8.0	1.0	—	—	—	—	—	—
Agriculture only	192	30	19.0	14.0	12.0	9	7.0	5	4	—	—

the midnineteenth century, farmers were likely to own real property in more equitable portions than were nonfarmers. No doubt, then, wealth distribution for American society at large became increasingly unequal during the first one-half of the nineteenth century as more and more communities turned toward manufacturing and commerce and away from agriculture. Nevertheless, it should be remembered that most Americans still lived in rural areas in 1860.[6]

Wealth distribution may be a function of economic activity, but in a larger sense both distribution and activity are probably best understood in terms of hierarchical location. It will be recalled that a community's location in an urban hierarchy affects both type and scale of economic activity. Upper- and middle-level places contain larger and more diverse commercial operations than lower ones and attract manufacturing firms, lawyers, and other professionals not ordinarily found elsewhere. Precisely these activities promote inequality. Therefore, upper-level places may be expected to possess less equitable distributions than would lower ones. Indeed, distribution should vary from less to more nearly equal as one moves from top- to upper- to middle- to lower-level places. In fact, this progression appears characteristic of our data with ownership highly centralized in Boston and Worcester, less so in Northampton, and relatively equal in Pelham (table 5.4). Taken from Edward Pessen's *Riches, Class, and Power*, data for Boston are from an earlier date and are not strictly comparable with our own. Still, in 1848, Boston wealth was owned in very unequal portions which apparently became less equal in the next few years and thus, by 1860, approximated or perhaps surpassed the level of inequality in Worcester. Distributions in other places such as New York and Philadelphia appear roughly comparable to Boston's, so that it seems likely that such cities possessed the least equitable distributions of property of any communities in America.[7]

Towns such as Northampton and hamlets like Pelham show substantially less concentration of wealth than do Boston and Worcester, so the relationship between hierarchical location and wealth distribution appears to work quite well. However, this scheme should not be pushed too far since idiosyncratic factors and unique economic advantages such as Ware's waterpower and Salem's commercial heritage and proximity to the sea produced economic development which led to unequal ownership. Overall, then, wealth distribution, economic activity, and hierarchical location appear closely related, with idiosyncratic factors complicating the relationship. Commerce and manufacturing in upper- and middle-level places produced great inequalities of wealth which tapered off in lower-level hamlets. Agriculture produced greater equality, and the only communities approaching equitable distribution of property were low-level, less developed rural hinterlands.

Wealth Distribution and Age

Wealth and age were not linked in any simple fashion. A quick visual inspection of our data shows that rank-order correlation between these two variables was very low. It is true that younger men tended to be unpropertied and older ones well-to-do, but no regular overall relationship prevailed. Some young men had attained substantial wealth while many elderly people remained without property. Middle-aged men ranged from rich to poor. Most of the very rich people were in their forties and fifties.

Nor did men of similar ages own similar amounts of property. Table 5.5 presents the portion of wealth owned by the richest decile within each of five age cohorts. Except for the 16 to 30 year olds, wealth tended to be owned more equally among men of like age than in the population at large. Nevertheless, if most men of like age owned similar amounts of property we would expect the richest decile to own 30% to 40% of the wealth. Only in Pelham do such figures

TABLE 5.4

Hierarchic Level and Property Distribution
(% of total wealth owned in each group)

	Richest 1%	Richest 2–4%	Richest 5–15%	16%–100%
Top level				
Boston, 1848	37	27	32	4

	Decile Distribution									
	Richest								Poorest	
	(1)	(2)	(3)	(4)	(5)	(6)	(7)	(8)	(9)	(10)
Upper level										
Worcester, 1860	87	11.0	2	0.5	—	—	—	—	—	—
Middle level										
Northampton, 1860	72	19.0	8	1.0	—	—	—	—	—	—
Lower level										
Pelham, 1860	28	20.5	16	11.0	9	8	5	2	0.2	—

pertain. In the other towns, the richest 10% within each group typically owned 50% or more of the property.

The difficulty with age-wealth correlations and the reason for inequality within age cohorts lie in the presence of rich and poor men at all ages—that is, in the presence of the two groups which we have designated as the elite and the casualties. The significance of elite persons for social structure depends on their antecedents. Were they born rich or were they self-made men? These issues are taken up in chapter 6. For the casualties, the problem is less complex. These men who could not accumulate property as they aged were ill served by a society which was closed to them. Thus, our original question might be rephrased in the negative. What portion of society was cut off from opportunity and was unable to accumulate more than tiny amounts of property?

Table 5.6 shows the relative size of elite, middle, and casualties for men over age 30. The proportion of casualties seems distressingly high, with about one-half the men in Ware and Worcester failing to gain even minimal wealth holdings. In these two communities, given to manufacturing, wealth distribution was not simply a function of age and achievement, for the possibility of property ownership appears to have been closed to a very high proportion of their residents.

How are we to judge these figures concerning casualties? Certainly they belie the idea of a middling society characterized by widespread and readily available opportunity. In Ware and Worcester, more men over age 30 had failed than gained access to society. Even Northampton's 38% and Pelham's 34% seem high. Society can be called open only if we ignore one-third to one-half of the men over

TABLE 5.5
Wealth Distribution within Age Cohorts
(% of total wealth owned by richest decile)

	N	Whole pop.	Aged 16–30	Aged 31–40	Aged 41–50	Aged 51–60	Aged 61–
Northampton	1,061	72	88.0	79	49	45	64
Worcester	1,902	87	99.5	73	66	63	56
Ware	945	71	89.0	55	61	38	47
Salem*	—	—	—	—	—	—	—
Pelham	202	28	71.0	25	25	29	23

* Data unavailable for Salem.

TABLE 5.6

Social Groups in 1860 among Males Over Age 30
(% of total population in each group)

	N	Elite	Middle	Casualty*
Northampton	633	7	55	38
Worcester	1,044	8	38	54
Ware	569	2	48	50
Salem†	—	—	—	—
Pelham	147	0	66	34

* Casualties were men aged over 30 who did not own real and personal property valued over $749.
† Data unavailable for Salem.

age 30 who could not accumulate property. Did wealth distribution reflect an open society given to achievement in which ownership was a function of age? Only to a limited extent—at most, for one-half to two-thirds of the males over age 30.

The data in table 5.6 also suggest the importance of economic activity in determining the relative size of elite, middle, and casualties. Note the disproportionate percentage of casualties in Worcester and Ware, large middle in Pelham and Northampton, and oversized elite in Northampton and Worcester. Manufacturing appears to have promoted casualties, agriculture encouraged the middle, while activities in middle- and upper-level sites stimulated the growth of an elite. Such conclusions confirm the chapter's earlier findings on property ownership and economic activity and point to the powerful effect of hierarchical location on wealth distribution.

✑ 6 ❧

Property Mobility and Group Status

CHAPTER 6 CONTINUES the examination of social structure begun in the two preceding chapters. Our concern here is to understand property mobility and to bring some greater order to our findings. The first part of the chapter briefly reviews the ideas and data presented thus far and develops a model of communal social structure. The second portion examines property and geographic mobility, that is, the degree to which individuals were able to improve their economic and group status.

In chapters 4 and 5, we discovered very high rates of geographic mobility and great inequalities in property ownership. Mobility and inequality within the five towns existed in proportions similar to those discovered elsewhere and at levels which have led some scholars to posit a relatively closed or "nondemocratic" social system, characterized by widespread disorder. However, we argued that such conclusions seem premature. Using age, wealth, geographic mobility, and a hypothetical life cycle, we defined two sectors within each town's population and offered alternate explanations for mobility and inequality. Composed of elite and middle groups, the stable sector was made up of propertied and older people who remained in town over long periods of time. Their continuing presence offered elements of cohesion in the face of rapid population turnover among members of the young and casualty groups in the mobile sector.

The relative sizes of the four groups and of the stable and mobile sectors were a function of urbanization, hierarchical location, and economic activity. Relationships among these various factors (i.e., group and sector size, geographic mobility, inequality, economic activity) can be systematized into a model which describes the basic

FIGURE 6.1
A Social Model

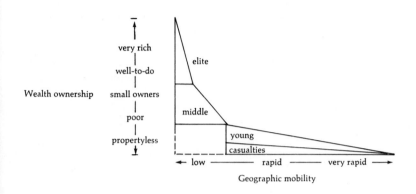

Geographic mobility

contours of midnineteenth-century social structure (figures 6.1 and 6.2). In figure 6.1, wealth is plotted along the vertical axis and geographic mobility on the horizontal one. Thus, someone located toward the upper left portion of the figure would be affluent and unlikely to migrate and someone at the lower right would be poor or propertyless and very mobile. Propertied and relatively immobile, members of the elite and middle groups formed the stable sector toward the upper left part of the figure while poor or propertyless and highly migratory members of the young and casualties fell into the mobile sector toward the lower right.

A brief examination of the figure will give a general understanding of communal social structure. For example, an extended vertical axis indicates great inequality stemming from a large elite or expanded young and casualty groups or both. Looking at the figure, then, we can quickly determine the level of inequality and the degree to which it was the result of a large rich group or expanded poor or property-less ones. Similarly, the figure can be used to ascertain the extent and sources of geographic mobility.

In addition to providing a simple visual description of the compo-nents of social structure, the model can be used to portray variations among communities (figure 6.2). In an upper-level city such as Worcester, the model's vertical and horizontal axes are extended. The elite, young, and casualty groups and mobile sector are expanded, but the middle group and stable sector are contracted. In a parochial hamlet such as Pelham which had no elite, a large middle, and small numbers of young and casualties, the axes are shortened. With a large middle, Northampton fell between these communal types, as shown in figure 6.2.

The remainder of chapter 6 seeks to determine the degree to which men were able to move about within the structure portrayed by the model. We particularly wish to know how often men were able to move up *and* to the left. Our strategy here is somewhat unusual. We are not measuring social mobility as it has been customarily defined but are rather concerned with the extent to which men stopped moving and were able to improve their real estate holdings. Did young men commonly move into the middle as they aged? Were casualties really casualties? What were the backgrounds of members of the elite? And, overall, to what extent did location and economic mix affect the answers to these questions?[1]

How Much Movement Up and to the Left Took Place?

Based on the federal censuses for 1850 and 1860, table 6.1 examines changes in real estate ownership for all males aged 31 to 60. Tax records were used in Salem. According to our model life cycle, all these men should have been settling in and accumulating wealth so everyone, including out-migrants, is taken into account. This procedure differs from other mobility studies, and it should be remembered that we are interested in movement up *and* left, not simply up.

As shown in the first three columns of table 6.1, most men died or left town and many of those who remained continued to own similar

FIGURE 6.2

Location in an Urban Hierarchy and the Social Model

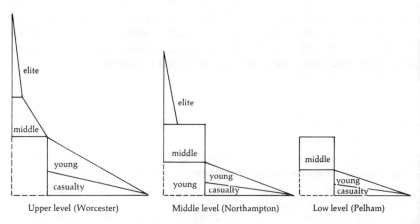

amounts of real estate in 1850 and 1860. Roughly 80% of all men fall into these categories, so the vast majority of the five towns' males over age 30 did not move up and to the left. Nevertheless, some 11% to 14% did improve their real estate holdings by $1,000 or more, and about 5% rose out of the ranks of the unpropertied.

Outside of Pelham, variations among the towns were minimal except for the relative sizes of the geographically mobile and "no change" groups. Given other differences found among the towns, the similarity of rates of real property mobility is surprising and will be examined in more detail below. For the moment, though, we can be sure that a very limited portion of the populace attained property mobility as we have defined it. Looked at from this perspective, society seems remarkably closed.

We will call those men who improved their real estate holdings by $1,000 or more climbers or successful men. In all communities, about 60% of the climbers already owned real estate in 1850. During the next ten years, these men simply increased already existing holdings.

TABLE 6.1

Changes in Real Estate Ownership, 1850–1860:
Males over Age 30 (% in each group)

	N	Out-migrated or died	Holding same amount real estate (within $500 of 1850)	With real estate de-creasing $1,000 or more	With real estate in-creasing $1,000 or more	Moving from unprop-ertied to prop-ertied
Northampton	589	68	11	4	14	5
Worcester	695	70	12	4	12	4
Ware	428	63	20	3	11	5
Salem	667	60	22	3	11	5
Pelham	125	55	30	6	3	4

NOTE: Added horizontally, the percentages for each town do not equal 100. This is because men who underwent gains or losses between $500 and $999 are excluded and because propertyless men who gained by $1,000 or more would be counted twice (i.e., in columns 5 and 6). Tables 6.4–6.7 have these same characteristics. Property data for Salem are from tax records throughout this chapter.

Most of the successful men were between 31 and 50 years old, so the "typical" upward migrant was a property holder in his thirties or forties regardless of where he lived.

Even though intercommunal rates of property mobility were relatively equal and despite the general tendency for climbers to be propertied men aged 31–50, differences can be found in absolute levels of increases in real property ownership (table 6.3) and in the occupations of successful men (table 6.2). Most improved holdings were gained in dynamic, expanding areas of local economies and in service and construction trades but seldom occurred in manufacturing except at entrepreneurial levels. Roughly one-half the climbers in Northampton and Ware engaged in farming; 64% of Salem's successful men gained their living from shipping, leather working, or mercantile-business activities; and two-thirds of Worcester's climbers worked as farmers, businessmen, manufacturers, or builders (table 6.2). Climbers thus prospered in somewhat different occupations depending on their residence.

Absolute levels of property mobility varied substantially among the towns (table 6.3). Worcester climbers tended to rise much farther than those in the other communities. Seventy-three percent of the successful men in this place rose by at least $2,500 and 24% climbed $7,500 or more. Upwardly mobile men in Northampton and Salem

TABLE 6.2

Occupations of Men Who Increased Their Real Estate Holdings by $1,000 or More (% in each group)

		Occupational Category as of 1850							
	N	Farm	Business	Prof.	Mfg.	Leather	Building	Shipping	Other
Northampton	82	50	10	4	2	—	9	—	24
Worcester	83	20	18	6	16	—	13	—	27
Ware	47	45	13	2	4	—	9	—	28
Salem*	73	—	32	3	1	18	8	14	25
Pelham	4	—	—	—	—	—	—	—	—

* Data for Salem are from the 1850 federal census and tax records for 1850 and 1860.

TABLE 6.3

Absolute Levels of Increased Real Estate Holdings,
1850–1860 (% of men in each group)

	N	Low ($1,000–2,499)	Medium ($2,500–7,499)	High ($7,500–)
Northampton	82	44	39	17.0
Worcester	83	27	49	24.0
Ware	47	64	28	8.5
Salem*	73	49	40	11.0

* Data for Salem are from tax records for 1850 and 1860.

fared less well, but one-half or more of them fell into the medium
($2,500–$7,499) or high group ($7,500). However, most climbers in
Ware attained only low mobility ($1,000–$2,499) with but 36.5%
rising by $2,500 or more.

Whatever the level of mobility, the paths to success were more a
creation of opportunities generated by urban growth than a consequence of possibilities created directly by manufacturing. In part,
disproportionate numbers of farmers rose because so many of them
owned real estate to begin with, but agriculture greatly benefited from
expanding urban demand for meat, dairy products, and perishables.
Urban climbers grasped the significance of the need for goods and
services too and profited as butchers, grocers, storekeepers, victual-
lers, and the like. Other businessmen rose as a result of opportunities
created by hierarchical location and growing needs for raw materials.
For example, virtually all real estate gains in Salem depended on her
function as shipper and supplier of leather products, wood, and coal.
Finally, urban growth produced expanding chances for property acquisition in trades tied to construction.

Few factory workers climbed, and most improvements in real estate
holdings occurred outside manufacturing in areas of the local economy which were stimulated by the rise of cities and growing needs for
raw materials. Construction and service trades benefited but, outside
these two activities, the paths to success varied in relation to local
economic advantages and each community's function in the wider
economy.

Most men did not climb and society seems strikingly closed. But,
despite general similarities in rates of climbing, men living in different

communities attained varying levels of ascent and followed differing occupational routes to success.

How Often Did Young Men Move into the Middle?

Apparently most young men did not climb but slid on to become members of the group we have designated casualties (table 6.4). Seventy to eighty percent of the men aged 26 to 35 as of 1850 left town or died and another 10% or so failed to improve their real property holdings. Only about 10% of these men increased their real wealth by $1,000 or more while between 4% and 9% rose from among the unpropertied. We cannot be sure what happened to the out-migrants. No doubt some of them gained success elsewhere, but only a few (10–15%) of the young men gained entry into the middle group within the confines of their place of residence after 1850. These findings again suggest a relatively closed social system, and they raise serious doubts about our life cycle model. We will return to these issues in chapter 7.

Several interesting differences in rates of youthful mobility appear among the towns. Northampton and Ware show improved real estate holdings for about 12% of the young men—nearly double Worcester's 6%. This difference apparently stems from the greater importance of agriculture in the two former towns. Many of the young

TABLE 6.4

Changes in Real Estate Ownership, 1850–1860: Males Aged 26–35 as of 1850 (% of total in each group)

	N	Out-migrated or died	Holding same amount real estate (i.e., within $500 of 1850)	With real estate de-creasing $1,000 or more	With real estate in-creasing $1,000 or more	Moving from unprop-ertied to prop-ertied
Northampton	262	71	10	3	12	7
Worcester	539	79	13	1	6	4
Ware	244	75	10	1	11	6
Salem*	374	72	16	1	9	9
Pelham	42	69	24	5	0	5

* Data for Salem are from tax records for 1850 and 1860.

climbers in Northampton (45%) and Ware (33%) were farmers, but few young mobiles engaged in agriculture in Worcester (6%). We have already noted the high level of ascent among agriculturists who benefited from new market conditions and a general tendency to be property owners. Farming also appears to have been an occupation in which men commonly acquired property at an early age.

Occupational factors may also account for Salem's high (9%) rate of movement from unpropertied to propertied, though the linkage is not entirely clear. Mostly involved in maritime trades, many of Salem's young climbers engaged in an activity in which property could frequently be acquired at an early age. The reasons for this are obscure, but movement from the unpropertied may be due to the tendency of merchants and shippers to give their sons shipboard experience and to the proclivity of persons in maritime trades for making small speculations in their own right. In any case, occupational choice appears to have affected the life chances of young men.

These relationships among occupation, age, and property acquisition suggest that different occupations possessed varying life-cycle patterns depending on their own internal structure and logic. That is, the duration of apprenticeship, the time spent in learning skills, the chances for property accumulation, and the timing of it may all have been tied to occupation.

Were Casualties Really Casualties?

Most casualties either out-migrated, died, or remained as propertyless residents. Between 84% and 93% of the casualties fell into one of these categories (table 6.5)—a dismal record unsurpassed by any other group. Seldom climbing up and left, casualties skidded on without success and formed a distinctive group within the mobile sector.

Though most persisting casualties appear to have remained in their lowly station, some of them did rise. This important movement indicates that propertyless men over age 40 were not all doomed to living their lives in poverty and that they could still aspire to property ownership. Many of these successful casualties rose in occupations similar to those of the young men, but some engaged in low-skill work which set them apart from other climbers. No broad generalization can be made about success in these low-skill trades for we have too few cases to work with, but it seems likely that men working in such occupations attained real estate ownership at a later age than did men employed in more dynamic and skilled work. In other words, the life-cycle patterns of laborers, operatives, tailors, and the like were probably quite different from those of farmers, builders, storekeepers, and so on.

Were casualties really casualties? Apparently they were, or at least very few of them seem to have been able to struggle up and into the middle. Still, we cannot be sure about the careers of out-migrants, so a definitive answer to the question awaits further research.

Did Members of the Middle Group Customarily Rise?

In comparison with the young and casualties, members of the middle group did remarkably well. Approximately 20% of the middle improved their real holdings by $1,000 or more (table 6.6), and only about 50% out-migrated or died. Apparently, then, property mobility came more easily in the stable than the transient sector. Once someone had struggled out of the young or casualty groups into the stable sector, he found ascent less difficult than before.

More volatile than the young or casualties, the middle contained substantial movement down as well as up. Roughly 10% of the real estate holdings of middle-group men declined by $1,000 or more. The

TABLE 6.5

Changes in Real Estate Ownership, 1850–1860: Unpropertied Males Aged 41–50 as of 1850 (% of total in each group)

	N	Out-migrated or died	Holding same amount real estate (i.e., within $500 of 1850)	With real estate increasing $1,000 or more	Moving to propertied
Northampton	73	74	10	14	15
Worcester	114	74	18	9	9
Ware	64	69	22	8	11
Salem*	139	69	24	6	7
Pelham	5	—	—	—	—

* Data for Salem are from tax records for 1850 and 1860.

path to success was difficult, especially the climb out of the mobile sector into the stable one. Once there in the stable sector—in the middle—climbing became easier but the risk of sliding back increased too.

Almost all upward mobility in the middle group involved increases of less than $3,000 though a few merchants and manufacturers made gains of $10,000 or more. Occupations of middle-group climbers closely resemble those shown in table 6.2, with mobility taking place in dynamic areas of local economies. Indeed, it could hardly be otherwise, for the middle group provided many of the successful men who formed the basis for the calculations presented in that table.

For the most part, downwardly mobile members of the middle group engaged in vulnerable occupations: watchmen, laborers, operatives, and diverse artisans and skilled workers. Many of the middle-group men in these trades slid back to become casualties. That is, they lost their small property holdings and fell into the ranks of the poor or unpropertied. Owners of small amounts of real estate and engaged in insecure occupations, these men formed a distinctive part of the middle group. In this fringe area between middle and casualty, the risks were great and some men fell back.

Overall, the middle seems to have been much more open than was

TABLE 6.6

Changes in Real Estate Ownership, 1850–1860: Men Aged 31–60
Who Owned Real Estate Valued between $750 and $9,999
(% of total in each group)

	N	Out-migrated or died	Holding same amount real estate (i.e., within $500 of 1850)	With real estate decreasing $1,000 or more	With real estate increasing $1,000 or more
Northampton	278	53	13	7	19
Worcester	253	50	11	12	25
Ware	176	49	23	7	16
Salem*	198	33	22	13	23
Pelham	103	51	33	8	2

* Data for Salem are from tax records for 1850 and 1860.

society at large. Men in the middle did rather well for themselves even though a few skidded downward into the ranks of the casualties.

What Were the Origins of Members of the Elite?

In the preceding analysis of casualties, the young, the middle, and general property mobility, we focused on men's careers between 1850 and 1860. Did they leave town or die during these ten years, gain or lose wealth, or move from unpropertied to propertied status? With the elite, our interest is somewhat different in that we want to discover elite backgrounds, not what happened to them between 1850 and 1860. Analysis begins with a group of wealthy men in 1860 and traces them backward in time. Where did they come from? What were their social and economic backgrounds? Nevertheless, before turning to the question of origins, it does seem worthwhile to subject the 1850 elite to the same procedures used with the other three groups.

Table 6.7 examines changes in real property ownership among men between 31 and 60 years of age who held real estate valued at $10,000 or more in 1850. Between 39% and 50% of these elite men left town or died in the ten years after 1850. These figures are approximately the same as those for the middle—an indication that out-migration was related to property ownership itself rather than the amount owned. However, members of the elite were much more likely to expand their holdings than were persons in the middle or any other group. Rates of property mobility for the elite were about twice as large as those for the middle and three times as great as those among the young and casualties. Furthermore, the absolute amount of movement among the elite was substantially larger than that for the middle. Middle-group climbers typically gained $2,000 or $3,000, but members of the elite commonly leaped up several thousand dollars—often $10,000 or more. Owning more property, members of the elite moved up more readily and moved farther up when they did climb.

Elite origins are very difficult to trace, so the character of elite backgrounds cannot be precisely established. Nevertheless, evidence is not entirely lacking and some tentative conclusions may be hazarded. Most very rich men came from well-to-do or wealthy backgrounds. That is, most of the men valued at $100,000 or more on the 1860 census or tax rolls can be traced, and even though many of them had clearly added to the family fortune, most had not risen far—certainly very few climbed from poverty to riches. The Pickmans and Silsbees of Salem could trace their fortunes to the eighteenth century, as could the Lincolns, Paines, and Salisburys of Worcester and the Clarks of

Northampton. Still, even among the very rich, a few newcomers could be found who had risen from poverty and made their money in a single generation. George Peabody made his way out of humble circumstances to become one of Salem's richest men, and Ichabod Washburn of Worcester used mechanical genius to rise from a penniless youth to great wealth.[2]

Beneath the very rich, among men owning property valued between $25,000 and $100,000, upward mobility was more common. Communal variations also begin to appear at this level. In Worcester, many men climbed from the lowest levels of the middle group to the upper reaches of the elite. Several had been born to poor parents. Indeed, careful reading of biographies of Worcester's successful men suggests that upward mobility of these proportions was commonplace in that town during the 1840s and 1850s. Several factors account for the high level of movement into Worcester's elite. Worcester developed very rapidly between 1840 and 1860, and the economic spinoff from this development tended to remain within the town, thus continuously spawning new opportunities. Furthermore, most of these opportunities were at a technological and organizational level where commonsensical mechanical skills and small amounts of capital could generate very profitable and readily expandable businesses. Thus, ambitious young men with mechanical skills often rose to affluence. In fact, most

TABLE 6.7

Changes in Real Estate Ownership, 1850–1860: Men Owning More Than $9,999 in Real Estate as of 1850 (% of total in each group)

	N	Out-migrated or died	Holding same amount real estate (i.e., within $500 of 1850)	With real estate decreasing $1,000 or more	With real estate increasing $1,000 or more
Northampton	16	50	0	13	38
Worcester	39	44	0	15	41
Ware	2	50	0	0	50
Salem*	36	39	6	17	36
Pelham	0	—	—	—	—

* Data for Salem are from tax records for 1850 and 1860.

successful young men did not make it on their own but were aided by gifts from parents or loans from wealthy men, temporary partnerships with older, more established businessmen, and by inexpensive rental of shops, equipment, and power in one of Worcester's industrial buildings. Of course, gifts, loans, partnerships, and rentals were only a special form of spinoff and reinvestment of profit, so the crucial factors contributing to high-level mobility into Worcester's elite remain rapid growth, location of spinoff, and the level of technological and organizational development.[3]

Salem, Northampton, and Ware did not possess the combination of factors which contributed to elite mobility in Worcester, so entry into the elite was much lower in these three towns. Dominated by activities tied to oceangoing commerce, Salem's economy was vertically integrated and just entering a period of major expansion in 1860. Except for tanning and currying, Salem's economic ventures involved large commitments of capital in ships, wharves, warehouses, factories, and machinery. In the leather trades, technology and organization apparently imposed upper limits as to size and productivity, so that most tanners or curriers were valued at less than $25,000 on Salem's 1860 tax rolls. Furthermore, a few families may still have dominated leather working to the point of restricting opportunities for most tanners and curriers. (The same surnames frequently recur among owners of tanning and currying shops.) All these factors— slow growth, vertical integration, need for capital, leather working technology and organization—combined to keep mobility into Salem's elite well below that of Worcester's.

Northampton's slow growth, her lack of transportation and slippage in New England's hierarchy of cities, her inadequate sources of power and overall limited economic development all restricted opportunities in that town. To be sure, a few men did climb from poverty to affluence in Northampton, but chances for marked upward mobility were not widely present except perhaps in agriculture. Even in farming, land tenure systems and technology prohibited large-scale rationalization and access to the sort of profits which could be made in Worcester's manufacturing shops.

Ware presented an even less promising situation than did Northampton. After a sudden spurt in the 1820s, no further growth took place in Ware and spinoff from her textile mills went out of town. Three men rose in activities linked to the mills and two mill owners greatly expanded their wealth, but no one else in Ware owned more than $10,000 in real estate.

These impressionistic conclusions can be subjected to a limited empirical analysis by tracing the rich men of 1860 back to the 1850 census. Ten years is too short a time to reveal very much, so we should not expect a great deal from this process, but some patterns may appear nevertheless. Eight men in the five towns held real estate valued at $100,000 or more in 1860. Six of these men owned real estate worth $30,000 or more in 1850, and the one man who rose from among the unpropertied belonged to the wealthy Washburn family in Worcester. Again, it would appear that the upper levels of society were relatively stable. However, beneath this top level, among the lesser rich, much more climbing took place. Only 37% of the men holding real estate valued between $10,000 and $99,999 owned real property worth $10,000 or more in 1850. Another 26% of 1860's lesser rich held property valued between $2,000 and $9,999 in 1850, and 11% of them had climbed to affluence from among 1850's unpropertied. However, most of those who had been without property in 1850 appear to have been members of well-to-do local families.[4]

Overall, most of the very rich men in 1860 had been wealthy ten years before, and most men in the lesser rich had at least been substantial property owners in 1850. But many of the lesser rich had climbed quite far even though many of those men who rose from no property to riches were young members of wealthy families.

Few significant variations in elite mobility appear among the towns. Ten years is too short a period to reveal intercommunal differences. Significantly, though, many of Worcester's rich men of 1860 were not present ten years before; 30% of them were newcomers, compared with 17% in Northampton, 16% in Ware, and 13% in Salem. Most of these wealthy newcomers seem to have owned substantial amounts of wealth before arriving in one of the four towns. They apparently moved in order to expand their opportunities, so their disproportionate tendency to enter a thriving place such as Worcester seems quite logical.

Was society open? For those at the bottom, it was not—only one person in ten at this level was able to climb. But above the young and casualties in the middle and lesser elite, circumstances appear to have been relatively flexible. At least property mobility seems to have been readily available to men who had made their way into the middle or lesser elite or who had been born into one of these groups. At the very top of society among the extremely rich, society again seems to have been closed—most people at this level had been born to affluence. Was society open? For men in the middle it was, but for those at the bottom it was not.

A Summary and Interpretation
of Social Structure

CHAPTER 7 CONCLUDES OUR examination of social structure with a summary and interpretation of all the materials presented thus far. This summary is based on the social model described in the previous chapter and seeks to integrate our findings on wealth distribution, geographic movement, and property mobility with what we know about economic development, hierarchical location, and life cycle.

The Social Model and Group Size in 1860

You will recall that our model used age, geographic mobility, and wealth ownership to define four social groups in a hierarchically organized society: an elite composed of wealthy men who owned real estate valued at $10,000 or more; a middle, formed by men over age 30 who held real property worth $750 to $9,999; the young aged 16 to 30 who owned real property valued at less than $750 or none at all; and casualties aged 31 to 60 who possessed less than $750 worth of real estate. Let's take the model and the four groups and look at them in more detail.

How large were the four groups in 1860, and what proportion of their members had lived in town for ten years or more? As shown in table 7.1, group sizes varied considerably among the towns. We've seen these patterns before in chapter 6, but their origins are worth reviewing. Offering commercial and professional opportunity, upper- and middle-level places (Worcester, Northampton) possessed expanded elites while agricultural communities with many farmers (Pelham, Ware, Northampton) had substantial middles. Manufacturing towns (all communities except Pelham) developed large young and casualty groups. Rapidly growing towns (Worcester, Salem) had more young men, and static places (Ware, Pelham) contained more casualties.

Resulting from variations in hierarchical location and economic development, these group configurations produced sharp inequalities and very high rates of geographic mobility. Elite and middle groups owned virtually all the wealth, and members of the young and casualties moved with astounding frequency. In Worcester, for example, the richest 10% of the population owned 87% of the wealth and 28% of the men moved out of town every year. As many as 100,000 people probably moved in and out of Worcester between 1850 and 1860, even though her total population never went over 25,000.

Historians finding similar levels of geographic mobility elsewhere have wondered how any social coherence at all could have been maintained in the face of such rapid movement. However, the situation appears less chaotic when we recognize that many members of the elite and middle had lived in town for several years and did not move much at all. Table 7.2 shows the proportions of each 1860 group which had been present ten years earlier in 1850. Tracing people backward in this fashion in order to establish their *priority* shows that a large majority of the middle and elite were long-time residents. Representing between 18% and 30% of the towns' populations, these two groups formed what we have previously designated the stable sector of the populace. Members of the stable sector held communities together despite high levels of mobility among the transients. No matter that many thousands of people moved in and out of town. Some had not moved at all. Indeed, members of the old core families who still populated the stable sector could trace their

---

TABLE 7.1
Group Sizes in 1860 (% in each group)

	N	Elite	Middle	Young	Casualty
Northampton	1,183	4	26	41	29
Worcester	1,910*	5	17	44	34
Ware	935	1	23	38	38
Salem	1,122*	2	16	47	35
Pelham	202	—	37	25	38

* Data for Worcester and Salem are based upon 25% samples.

TABLE 7.2
Priority: 1860 to 1850 (% present in each group)

	N	Elite	Middle	Young	Casualty
Northampton	340	79	68	5	19
Worcester	424	71	58	11	35
Ware	306	75	74	14	27
Salem	367	86	71	8	32
Pelham	100	—	56	33	33

NOTE: Discrepancies between data presented here and in chapter 4 should be recognized. See footnote, p. 38. I have used samples in each town: Northampton (33.3%), Worcester (10%), Ware (33.3%), Salem (10%), and Pelham (50%).

ancestry back several generations to the eighteenth century and before. Their presence offered a sense of permanence and history in otherwise rapidly changing communities.[1]

The general tendency for the 1860 elite and middle to have been present in 1850 and for the young and casualties to have been absent remains consistent among the towns, but one important intercommunal variation should be noted. Worcester attracted many more middle and elite outsiders than did any of the other towns. As a center of transportation, commerce, and economic opportunity, Worcester drew ambitious men from the surrounding area. Though some came only with dreams of success, many of these in-migrants appear to have come to Worcester with capital already in hand.

Vacancies in the Stable Sector

Economic development expanded the absolute size of the stable sector (i.e., the elite and middle groups). In 1850, Northampton's stable population contained 321 men, but this had grown to 546 in 1860. During the same period, Worcester's elite and middle expanded from 1,181 to 2,032, Ware's from 250 to 332, Salem's from 763 to 1,242, but Pelham's shrank from 104 to 86.* Expansion of this sort produced vacancies. For example, even if we assume that all 321 members of Northampton's stable population remained between 1850 and 1860, growth alone would have produced 225 new places in the middle and

* These figures were computed by projecting the percentages in table 7.1 against the adult male population in the 1860 federal census and should be seen as rough approximations.

elite by 1860 (table 7.3). But, of course, members of the 1850 stable population who died, moved, or skidded back created additional openings. Column 2 in table 7.3 shows the total number of vacancies produced by growth, skidding, death, and out-migration. At first sight, these openings may seem substantial in number. After all, Worcester had 1,442 vacancies, Salem 743, and Northampton 394. But a second glance, coupled with a review of migration figures, reminds us that many thousand men competed for what now seems a starkly limited number of opportunities to enter the stable sector.

Who filled these vacancies? Our pursuit of the answers to this question will be somewhat indirect and no firm empirically based conclusions can be established, so our arguments here should be seen as speculative. Table 7.4 examines the composition of the towns' stable populations in 1860. One-third or so of the members of the towns' 1860 stable populations had occupied a similar local status ten years before (column 2, table 7.4). Vacancies thus fell to a combination of newcomers and upwardly mobile 1850 residents. Pelham's figures seem anomalous, but elsewhere upper-level places drew greater proportions of outsiders. For example, 42% of the men in Worcester's 1860 stable sector were from outside town. The characteristics of these newcomers are hard to establish because our priority samples are too small to allow detailed analysis. Nevertheless, as of 1860 most newcomers were men between 35 and 50 years of age who engaged in business, construction, or manufacturing. Moving in midlife, these men had apparently already established stable group ties elsewhere and had relocated themselves in order to expand their businesses. Impressionistic evidence supports such conclusions about newcomers—at least we can find many biographies in the Worcester

TABLE 7.3
Vacancies in Stable Sector (N in each group)

	Net Vacancies (1860 stable pop. − 1850 stable pop.)	Total vacancies (net + those created by migration, etc.)
Northampton	225	394
Worcester	851	1,442
Ware	82	207
Salem	479	743
Pelham	− 18	34

County histories which follow the pattern outlined above. However, given the weakness of our evidence, these ideas about newcomers should be accepted as speculative rather than proven.

Vacancies not filled by newcomers were occupied by upwardly mobile residents. Again, because of our small sample, the precise characteristics of upwardly mobiles are difficult to establish. Most climbers as of 1860 were either young men in their late twenties or early thirties or men of middle age in their late forties and fifties. Young men followed diverse occupations—farming, construction, business, and professions—but older men tended to cluster in manual trades. Significantly, many of the young men first appear as members of propertied households in 1850. That is, they were sons of propertied men.

Our data are not very good here but they are consistent with findings in chapter 6 on property mobility among the young and casualties. Taken together, the data in chapter 6 and the arguments above suggest a *tracking* process through which men became involved in the social system in very different ways. Depending on the nature of this involvement and of the social system, a man's life chances varied markedly.

Born to security and opportunity, the sons of middle and elite

TABLE 7.4

Composition of Stable Sector (% of total in each category)

	N	From 1850 stable sector	Newcomers from outside	From upwardly mobile 1850 residents
Northampton	140	28	32	40
Worcester	224	29	42	29
Ware	106	38	26	36
Salem	167	40	28	32
Pelham	37	44	44	12

NOTE: I have sampled in each town: Northampton (33.3%), Worcester (10%), Ware (33.3%), Salem (10%), Pelham (50%). The Ns in the table are not those which would be expected given the sizes of the towns' stable sectors suggested in the preceding pages. This is apparently due to the way in which I calculated the sizes of the stable sector and to sampling error (I drew a sample not of the stable sector itself but of the whole population in order to compute table 7.2). The large discrepancy between actual and expected Ns in Salem is probably due to the illegibility of much of the 1860 federal census for Salem.

parents began the rush for success with a decided head start. They could plan their lives, learn useful skills, and move purposefully from place to place. No doubt parents provided household environments congenial to success and competitiveness, but more importantly they offered their sons capital—education, training, and money. Wills written in Northampton between 1800 and 1840 repeatedly refer to gifts of money presented to children (and grandchildren) when they first matured or left home. Northampton farmers often provided sons with land, and parents customarily arranged for their children to learn useful skills as carpenters, store clerks, and the like. Coupled with financial capital, such skills formed bases for success and continued middle-group status. Well-to-do parents also invested in education—often sending their sons to private academies and to Harvard or Yale. Though not particularly practical, education of this sort offered prestige, provided important personal connections, and eased entry into the professions.

Supported by these advantages, sons of middle and elite parents probably followed life-cycle patterns similar to the hypothetical one described in chapter 4. They moved about as young men, acquired skills, and settled in at age 30 or so as propertied members of the stable population. Perhaps they relocated in their forties to expand their opportunities, but by then they were established members of the stable population.

This tracking process did not produce inevitable success, for it was subject to all sorts of unforeseeable disruptions and detours. Luck certainly played a crucial role in people's economic lives, as did such impersonal forces as the business cycle and patterns of economic development. Inflexible skills could quickly become less useful, or even obsolete, as circumstances changed. Communal social and economic structure imposed upper limits on commercial and manufacturing ventures and determined the precise nature and extent of opportunity. For example, no matter how privileged and skilled he was, a man could not operate large stores or factories in a town like Northampton where transportation and the market could not support such extended businesses. Communal restrictions of this sort did not prohibit success or curb the impact of privilege or tracking, but they certainly influenced the level of achievement a man might realistically hope to attain.

In addition to establishing ceilings, communal structure patterned the careers of tracked individuals. In chapter 5, we noted a tendency for men's wealth to plateau at about age 40. This leveling off appears to have taken place in occupations and communities where the upper limits of opportunity were relatively low. In such situations, continued success demanded a change of residence or occupation or both. Most of the very successful men in our towns simply added occupations to the one in which they first made their money. Merchants went into banking, insurance, and real estate speculation. Manufacturers added new products or branched out into investments similar to those of the merchants.

Lacking advantages, poorly educated, less skilled, without financial support, many men began their lives on a very different track—one destined to lead most of them to become casualties. A few talented, ambitious, and lucky men who started without advantages fought their way up. Through great sacrifice, by middle age others clawed their way into the lower reaches of the stable sector. But they were vulnerable and often slid back. Still, most men beginning on this disadvantaged track stayed there and ended their lives among the casualties.

The basic ideas here are relatively simple and are familiar to anyone who has thought much about human society and behavior. Born to privilege, some men begin their lives with substantial advantages, but others must make their way without such aids. Luck, impersonal forces, socioeconomic context, specific talents, skills, and character traits—all influence the degree to which men prosper, but privileges certainly ease the way to success. For the most part, socioeconomic context does not determine whether a man will succeed, but it certainly does define both the range and upper potential of economic opportunity. We have seen, for example, how, in the 1840s and 1850s, Worcester's peculiar characteristics encouraged an entrepreneurial mobility largely unavailable in the other towns.

These ideas bear directly on our analysis of social structure. In 1860, the stable populations of the five towns appear to have been largely composed of people already tracked for middle or elite status. Many had belonged to the stable populations of ten years before, and the majority of the vacancies seem to have been filled by newcomers who had already gained middle status in another community or by young climbers of middle and elite backgrounds. Only a few upwardly mobiles and less skilled men who arrived in the stable sector late in life appear to have gotten there by a different route or from a different track.

Affecting relationships among social groups, occupations, wealth, and age, this tracking process can be observed in the towns' 1860 populations, but we must be careful here for we are seeking to derive descriptions of dynamic processes from static, cross-sectional data.

Farming and most nonmanual occupations show high proportions of stable sector members, while manual trades evidence very low percentages of middle and elite persons. In Worcester, for example, roughly one-half of the professionals and businessmen and two-thirds of the manufacturers had gained at least middle status, but only about one-eighth of the skilled workers and artisans were able to attain similar positions.

Such figures suggest that a young man entering a profession or business stood a relatively good chance of making his way into the middle group—that he was tracked for the stable sector. But they also point out that someone beginning as an unskilled laborer, artisan, or skilled laborer stood little chance of middle-group status and was more likely to slide on to become a casualty. In our Worcester sample, 398 young skilled laborers and artisans competed with 305 casualties to gain access to middle-group positions which only 102 of their fellow workers had already gained. Casualties outnumbered stable-group men by about 3 to 1. However, in the same town, 28 young businessmen struggled with 47 casualties to gain the same middle or elite positions acquired by 66 other businessmen. Stable-group businessmen outnumbered casualties by roughly 1.2 to 1. Certainly the young businessman stood a much greater chance of success than did his laboring counterpart. He was on a more promising track.

The nonmanual track itself may have been more promising, but many of the young men who engaged in business, manufacture, and the professions gained an additional advantage, for they had acquired wealth before age 30. Roughly one-third (Northampton 50%, Worcester 37%, Ware 27%, Salem 35%) of the men aged 30 or less who worked in one of these three kinds of occupations owned wealth valued at $500 or more, but only a tiny portion (Northampton 15%, the other towns 2%) of the young manual laborers had acquired similar amounts of real and/or personal property. These data are consistent with our suggestion that some men began their working lives with distinct advantages. We might guess that many of these young men in nonmanual occupations began their labors with a superior education, a well-placed clerkship, or some financial support from parents or other benefactor. Who filled vacancies in the stable sector? Apparently most were filled by men who were tracked for success.*

* Drawn from static data and grouping many occupations together, our description of the tracking process is simplistic. Occupations within the general categories manual and nonmanual certainly varied greatly from one another. Furthermore, many of the occupations themselves changed in response to economic

Summary and Conclusions

Our findings thus far relate to one of three broad themes: (1) location and economic development; (2) social structure; and (3) individual lives or life cycles. As aspects of a whole, these themes can be integrated into a cohesive description of society in midnineteenth-century New England. In the years between 1800 and 1860, improvements in transportation first altered and then solidified economic relationships among Massachusetts towns and cities. Cities located toward the upper end of the new system possessed high thresholds of opportunity—that is, they were communities in which large-scale commercial activity could take place. And, as focal points of transportation, they tended to attract manufacturing, financial institutions, and professional services. These activities existed at reduced scales and lower frequencies in middle-level towns and disappeared altogether in low-level rural hamlets.

Location in an urban hierarchy thus influenced both social structure and individuals. Affecting the nature and distribution of occupations, location imposed ceilings on individual careers. An ambitious man could rise only to the limits imposed by his residence and stood to gain more in a high-level as opposed to a low-level location. He could move to a higher-level community to fulfill his ambitions but would encounter increased competition there.

Location also affected those factors which we have designated as the crucial elements of social structure: wealth ownership, age distribution, and geographic mobility. As bases for large commercial ventures and factories, upper-level communities possessed more wealthy men than did lower ones, but large enterprises also brought many young, poor, and geographically mobile employees into upper-level areas. Upper-level places thus tended to have higher rates of geographic mobility and greater inequalities of wealth than did lower-level communities.

Idiosyncratic factors such as Ware's waterpower or Salem's commercial heritage complicated relationships between social structure and the urban hierarchy. For the most part, however, thresholds of

---

development. Communal and occupational contexts were dynamic in ways which our analysis of static data cannot show. We would understand the tracking process much better if we analyzed the interrelationships among wealth, age, geographic mobility, and economic development *within each occupation in each town*. A pioneering effort along these lines can be found in Clyde Griffen, "Workers Divided: The Effect of Craft and Ethnic Divisions in Poughkeepsie, New York, 1850–1880," in *Nineteenth Century Cities* (New Haven, 1969), pp. 49–97.

opportunity, levels of inequality, and rates of geographic mobility were high in upper-level cities, decreased in middle-level towns, and fell still more in low-level hamlets.

Location influenced occupational mix and placed ceilings on opportunity, but specific economic factors determined the character of the situation beneath those upper thresholds. Spinoff and profits that remained within their home community opened opportunity and stimulated economic growth. But, when profits were invested externally, a town was left without continuing bases for development.

Spinoff and growth played enormously important roles, for urban development itself generated more opportunities than did manufacturing. Construction and service trades flourished while farmers reaped harvests of profits in their efforts to feed rising numbers of city dwellers. In this curious but very important process, cities stimulated rural life. Cities may have produced large propertyless populations within their boundaries, but urban demands for foodstuffs encouraged farming in nearby areas and farming was an activity characterized by widespread property ownership and relatively equitable distributions of wealth. Urban growth thus had very different influences within and outside city boundaries.

In manufacturing, the greatest possibilities for upward mobility existed in technologically unsophisticated activities which were capable of rationalization but which were not yet highly capitalized or organized in large units. In such situations, common sense, relatively simple skills, and a little capital could eventually generate large and profitable businesses, but as more complex organization and technology were introduced, increased capital and training became necessary and opportunity fell off or at least changed markedly.

Location in an urban hierarchy is probably best seen as the determinate of overall structure, with specific economic conditions filling in details and influencing the ability of individuals to move about within the structure. Still, as we have seen, location and economic conditions were closely linked. In general, then, the most important single factor affecting our five towns was their place in an urban hierarchy, and that was a product of spatial location and transportation.

Regardless of location and economic activity, people living within the five towns varied from one another in age, wealth, and tendency to move. Some people, usually the young and propertyless, moved about with astounding frequency. But, at the core of society, holding it together, were older and propertied men who did not move much at all. Some members of this stable sector had lived in their communities for many years, a few could trace local roots back a generation or more, and most had been there for at least a decade. Peopling the town's institutions, owning its wealth, running its government, these stable residents were *the* community in so far as they perpetuated ongoing, patterned human relationships, both formal and informal.

Property mobility was common in the stable sector, with men often gaining $1,000 or more in real wealth between 1850 and 1860. However, few men climbed into the ranks of the very rich, so despite overall openness, the topmost reaches of the stable sector were relatively immune to penetration from below. Nevertheless, in optimal situations such as that in Worcester in the 1840s and 1850s, men of humble origins could gain substantial fortunes even if few of them joined the really wealthy.

Though the stable sector was open internally, the boundary between it and the transients was extremely difficult to cross. Most of the vacancies created by growth and out-migration were filled by men tracked for membership in the stable population rather than by transients from below. Stuck on a different track, most transients did not climb but tumbled on to join the group we have designated casualties.

Individuals confronted these social and economic realities with logic of their own—their ambitions, hopes, and fears. Given the nature of our data, we cannot find out what men thought and felt in the middle of the nineteenth century, but we can see patterns in men's lives whether conscious or not. The "normal" pattern in the stable group involved men in skill acquisition and geographic mobility until about age 30. Then, during the next few years, they settled in and began to accumulate property. Depending on location and occupation, this accumulation might plateau at about age 40 or continue upward until late in life. The plateau could be avoided by shifting or adding occupations or by migration.

Characteristic of men born into the stable sector, this life cycle depended on a tracking process which eased the way toward success. Our data are not very useful here and our conclusions are speculative, but it appears that some parents provided their children with advantages—"put them on the right track," as it were. Education, skills, and money allowed men born in the stable sector to begin their pursuit of wealth and security with a head start which helped them to settle in as the "normal" life cycle would have them do.

Lacking such advantages, less able to control their lives, most men followed rather different life cycles. Buffeted by circumstance, many of them continued to move throughout their lives without acquiring property or even minimal security. However, through great sacrifice and with some luck, a few of these less privileged men scrambled up into the stable sector. Usually arriving in the stable sector during their forties or fifties and vulnerable to uncertain employment, some of them slid back to transiency and propertylessness.

We may assume that older men who were still on the move—who had not gained property or security—must have felt powerless and alienated from a society which so little valued them and their efforts. However, we must be more tentative about the young men who may have remained optimistic about their life chances despite adversity and the examples of their elders. Since young people formed such a large portion of urban populations, the issue of their attitudes is very important, but without further research and better data we cannot be very sure what they thought about themselves or the society in which they lived.

What does this all mean? After seven chapters, what can we say about the nature of American society? Society was composed of two populations: the stable and the transient. On the run, transients had little prospect of success. For them, society was remarkably closed. But members of the stable sector prospered in a social system that was relatively open to them. Born to privilege and blessed with advantages, they and their kin filled the institutions that held communities together. They were American society as we usually know it.

Beyond these very broad generalizations, an element of relativity must be introduced. Transportation, hierarchical location, and economic circumstances determined the basic structure of the communities in which Americans lived. And the structure affected people's life chances. How was wealth distributed? How much geographic mobility took place? These and similar questions cannot be answered for society at large. The answers depend on where one looks.

ᄵ 8 ᄽ

Political Power

CHAPTER 8 DEPARTS FROM our examination of community structure to focus on power within the five towns. The latter parts of the chapter look at power in a broad sense and briefly analyze some general patterns of political dominance and subordinance, but our initial and major concern is with power in the narrow context of local politics. Overall, we want to discover the degree to which social and economic change during the first one-half of the nineteenth century provoked, or was accompanied by, shifts in the locus of political power within the five towns. But, more specifically, in the first part of the chapter we would like to find out: To what extent did the relative wealth of officeholders change between 1800 and 1854? To what degree did the occupations of officeholders shift between 1800 and 1854? (i.e., priority and family background) of officeholders change between 1800 and 1854? And, finally, how were shifts in power related to the general social and economic characteristics of the five towns?[1]

Wealth and Officeholders

Did the relative wealth of officeholders change between 1800 and 1854? Yes, it did. Officeholders tended to come from lower economic strata between 1845 and 1854 than they had a half century earlier. In both the early and middle parts of the nineteenth century, officeholding was the province of the well-to-do (table 8.1). In each period, most public officials were in the richest two deciles of the population regardless of their communal affiliation. We could hardly have expected otherwise, since virtually all studies of local political power have found officeholders to have been drawn from middle and upper social strata. Let's look at wealth and officeholding in greater detail.

Table 8.2 shows the percentage of officeholders in various deciles of
the propertied populace and the proportion of officials who did not
own property at all. Between 1800 and 1809, most officeholders came
from the very upper levels of the propertied (stable) sector of society
(table 8.2). More than one half the selectmen and clerks in Northamp-

TABLE 8.1
*Officeholders and Wealth (% of holders in the richest
two deciles of the adult male population)*

	N	1800–1809	N	1845–1854
Northampton	19	59	24	73.0
Worcester	11	73	148	69.5
Ware	23	22	22	86.0
Salem	23	74	135	67.0
Pelham	27	52	22	41.0

TABLE 8.2
*Officeholders and Wealth (% of holders in various deciles
of the propertied population or among the unpropertied)*

	N	1	2–3	4–10	Unpropertied	Unknown
Northampton						
1800–1809	19	53.0	37.0	10.5	0	0
1845–1854	24	17.0	37.5	29.0	0	17
Worcester						
1800–1809	11	54.5	18.0	18.0	0	9
1845–1854	148	24.0	25.0	21.0	22	8
Ware*						
1800–1809	23	9.0	22.0	26.0	0	43
1845–1854	22	23.0	27.0	41.0	0	9
Salem						
1800–1809	23	57.0	39.0	0.0	0	4
1845–1854	135	10.0	29.0	25.0	21	15
Pelham						
1800–1809	27	33.0	33.0	22.0	4	7
1845–1854	22	18.0	18.0	27.0	9	27

* Ware data for 1800 are incomplete as are Pelham's for 1845.

ton, Worcester, and Salem were from the richest decile of the propertied men. Less than 20% of the officials came from the fourth to tenth deciles. None were unpropertied even though men who did not own wealth were eligible for local office. However, a half century later, between 1845 and 1854, men in the wealthy first decile held office much less frequently. In Salem, for example, the proportion of wealthy officeholders had dropped from 57% to 10%. In addition, many more officials could be found in the fourth to tenth deciles, and, significantly, a large new group of propertyless city officers had appeared in Salem and Worcester.

Following a very different pattern from that of the other towns, the economic status of Ware's town officers improved. This increased affluence reflects the entry of well-to-do men associated with the Ware mills and their dominance of the community. Pelham town

TABLE 8.3

Occupations of Officeholders (% officeholders in each group)

	N	Farm	Merchant/ prof.	M
Northampton				
1800–1809	19	26	31.5	
1845–1854	24	42	17.0	1
Worcester				
1800–1809	11	18	45.0	
1845–1854	148	14	20.0	1
Ware*				
1800–1809	23	52	4.0	
1845–1854	22	45	18.0	1
Salem				
1800–1809	23	0	39.0	
1845–1854	135	0	30.0	
Pelham†				
1800–1809	27	74	0.0	
1845–1854	22	50	0.0	

* Data for Ware, 1800–1809, are incomplete. The percentage of farmers was ably much higher than 52.

† Data for Pelham, 1845–1854, are incomplete. The percentage of farmer probably well above 50.

officers continued to be drawn from a wide spectrum of society, though fewer of the larger farmers appear to have held office during 1845–1854. The many "unknowns" in Pelham no doubt reflect the town's general decline and a high level of out-migration.

Occupations of Officeholders

The occupations of officeholders slipped downward between 1800 and 1854 in much the same fashion as their wealth, but, for the most part, they continued to be middle level or above. As shown in table 8.3, most early nineteenth-century public officials in Worcester and Salem came from the ranks of merchants, lawyers, businessmen, and (in Salem) ship captains. In Salem, only three well-to-do artisans held office, and in Worcester no artisan or skilled laborer was chosen for

Business	White collar	Skilled labor/ artisan	Ship captain	Unknown
16	0	16	0	10.5
17	0	8	0	4.0
27	0	0	0	9.0
13	8	24	0	3.0
22	0	0	0	22.0
5	0	5	0	9.0
13	0	13	26	9.0
22	7	30	4	3.0
22	0	4	0	0.0
5	0	18	0	27.0

selectman or clerk. However, by midcentury, many artisans and skilled workers held office, and merchants, professionals, and ship captains were less frequently elected than they had been before. This shift downward was accompanied by changes which were more sideways or at least not as far down—note the election of men in manufacturing and white-collar trades at midcentury. In all, these two sorts of changes were quite substantial. In Worcester, manufacturers, white-collar men, artisans, and skilled workers occupied one-half the offices between 1845 and 1854 but had not held a single position 50 years before. Though less dramatic, similar changes took place in Salem.

In general, then, in the two larger communities the occupations of public officials changed substantially, with artisans, manufacturers, skilled laborers, and white-collar persons growing in influence while farmers, professionals, merchants, and ship captains lost power.

Northampton witnessed a much lower level of change. To be sure, manufacturers expanded their influence there, but artisans actually lost power and the great majority of offices remained in the hands of merchants, professionals, and farmers. Ware officeholding appears to have changed rather less than might have been expected, with the primary shifts being from farmers and innkeeper-businessmen to manufacturers, merchants, and professionals. (Note, however, that the proportion of farmers, 1800–1809, was undoubtedly higher than 52%.) And the figures for Ware in table 8.3 further underestimate change since members of the new occupations were frequently reelected while farmers customarily sat for only one year. Merchants, manufacturers, and professionals actually occupied a majority of the offices between 1845 and 1854, while farmers held only 22% of them even though farmers provided 45% of the officeholders. Many of the occupations of Pelham officeholders are unknown, so we cannot be very sure about changes there, though our data suggest that farmers and innkeepers lost power while artisans gained.

Table 8.4 summarizes the overall level of change in the occupations of public officials in the five towns. The numbers in the table represent the percentage of midcentury officeholders who came from occupational groups that did not hold office during the early nineteenth century. Officeholder occupations changed very little in Northampton (29%) but shifted substantially in Worcester (53%) and the other three towns. Salem's 40% change seems out of line with other information we have about the town and, in fact, is misleading. Well-to-do and self-employed, Salem's three early nineteenth-century artisan-selectmen included a ship chandler, a cooper, and a cabinetmaker, but the artisans and skilled laborers who held office at midcentury were largely unpropertied employees. The three artisans of 1800–1809 and the several workingmen of 1845–1854 thus did not relate to the local economy in the same ways even though members of both groups were ostensibly workingmen or artisans. The labels were the same but the nature of work performed and the level of personal autonomy were not. Taking these factors into account, the occupations of Salem officeholders appear to have changed more than 40% and probably approached or surpassed Worcester's 53%. Comparable adjustments do not have to be made in Northampton and Pelham, where artisan officials remained of a similar character in 1800 and 1854.

Social Status of Officeholders

Between 1800 and 1854, the social status (i.e., priority and family background) of officeholders appears to have changed substantially in Worcester, Pelham, and Ware but to have remained somewhat stable in Salem and quite stable in Northampton. Unfortunately, however, our data are too scattered and incomplete to allow precise measurement and comparison.[2]

In chapter 2, we noted the presence of several core families in each of the five towns in 1800. Locally resident for at least two generations, these families provided a continuing base for each town's stable population. In the early nineteenth century, members of these families often held local political office. They supplied almost three-quarters of the officials in Northampton (74%), about one-half in Worcester (45%), Pelham (48%), and Ware (52%), and just under one-third of the officeholders in Salem (30%).

TABLE 8.4
Overall Change in Officeholder Occupations

	% of officeholders from new groups
Northampton	29
Worcester	53
Ware	47
Salem	40
Pelham	41

By the middle of the century, members of these same core families had lost their political clout everywhere except in Northampton. Between 1845 and 1854, 18% of the officials in Ware and 23% in Pelham were descendants of the core families. But in Northampton, 37.5% of the town officers had core family ties. And many of the other officials in Northampton had old local connections, though not with a core family. Among those not members of a core family, 33% of Northampton's officeholders during 1845–1854 belonged to families that had been present in town in 1800. Overall, then, 70% of the men who held office in Northampton were either core family members or had 50-year-old local family connections. Neither Ware (27%) nor Pelham (36%) officeholders evidenced similar levels of old local ties. Family thus seems a peculiarly influential factor in Northampton.

It is difficult to establish family and old local ties for the many officials in the two larger cities, but apparently they remained significant in Salem and became relatively unimportant in Worcester. Core families lost influence in both places. Only 7% of the midcentury officials in Worcester and 19% in Salem were born in town and possessed a core family surname. But most officials in Salem did have established local roots: 62% of them had been born in town and 98% had lived in town for several (eight or more) years before taking office. In contrast, many Worcester officers appear to have been relative newcomers. Only 18% had been born in that city and a remarkable 33% of Worcester's city officials (1845–1854) had arrived in that city after 1844. Just 2% of Salem's officials arrived after 1844.

Summary: Officeholding, Wealth, Occupation, and Social Status

Three changes took place in all of the towns: (1) the relative wealth of officeholders declined, (2) their occupational status shifted downward or sometimes sideways, and (3) fewer officials belonged to the core families of 1800. Nevertheless, most public officials continued to come from middle social strata or above. Beyond these broad and commonly shared traits, changes in the locus of power varied considerably among the towns. Let us look briefly at each town in turn.

In Pelham, most officials were farmers of moderate wealth who did not have old local ties. Just over one-third of the officeholders had family connections to Pelham going back more than 50 years. In Ware, dominance fell into the hands of relatively affluent newcomers

—men who were associated with the factories or the small, new commercial center. Only about one-quarter of the officials had 50-year local kin connections.

Members of Salem's great commercial families left town after 1800, but town-born men retained a great deal of influence. Sixty-two percent of the Salem officeholders were born in that community. Nevertheless, few officeholders engaged in maritime trades, and many unpropertied artisans became public officials. Northampton shows even more continuity than Salem. Political power there stayed in the hands of men who worked as merchants, professionals, or farmers and who were either members of core families or had local kin ties of at least 50 years' duration.

The locus of political power changed more in Worcester than in any of the other four communities. Seldom born in town and frequently recent arrivals, few Worcester officers had old local connections. And, by midcentury, many of Worcester's officials were manufacturers or unpropertied workingmen. These intercommunal variations are summarized in table 8.5 and should be kept firmly in mind. They form the basis for the remainder of this chapter.

Power and Socioeconomic Context

In what ways were shifts in power related to the general social and economic characteristics of the five towns? Involving so many factors, the question can be more easily answered in a somewhat revised form: Which social and economic factors contributed to political continuity or discontinuity? Continuity and discontinuity here represent poles on a continuum rather than dichotomous variables, and it will be noted below that discontinuity had several different forms.

In order to persevere between 1800 and 1854, members of politically dominant groups had to be skilled, resourceful, relatively affluent, and internally cohesive. In 1800, political leaders in both Northampton and Worcester possessed most of these characteristics, but those in Ware, Pelham, and Salem did not (recall the discussion in chapter 2). Split by family and personal conflicts and divided into savagely competing factions, Salem's leaders were in no position to solidify their power. Neither were the hilltown farmer-officeholders of Pelham and Ware, who lacked the skill and wealth to maintain their control. Possessed of all the crucial traits to some degree, Worcester's leaders were men of wealth and ability who seem not to have squabbled among themselves, but they belonged to a new group which did not have any long-term stability since it had been founded just 20 years before, during the ferment after the Revolutionary War. Long established and powerful, Northampton's old-family elite had many very able and wealthy members who were ideally situated to maintain their influence and power.

Regardless of their own characteristics, members of dominant groups could only persevere if they found ongoing economic opportunity within the local community which was profitable, interesting, and suited to their talents. These opportunities also had to be attractive in relation to chances for advancement elsewhere. To argue in this fashion is only to suggest that skilled and talented members of dominant groups had to remain within the local community and had

TABLE 8.5

Summary of Changes in the Characteristics of Officeholders

	Wealth	*Occupation*	*Social status (core family influence declines everywhere)*
Northampton	General decrease in wealth	Little change; increase in mfg. and farm	Relatively stable; core family and other local ties strong
Worcester	General decrease in wealth; increase in unpropertied	Increase artisans and manufacturers	Unstable; many newcomers and very recent arrivals
Ware	Overall increase in wealth	Possible decline farm; increase mfg. and commercial	Many newcomers associated with factories and town center
Salem	General decrease in wealth; increase in unpropertied	Increase workingmen; decrease maritime	Relatively stable; many long-term residents
Pelham	General decrease in wealth	Little change; possible decline farm	Many newcomers

to prosper if they were to retain control or influence. If they did not prosper, they lost their capacity for dominance, and if they found external opportunity so attractive that they left, their influence would be felt elsewhere. However, very high levels of opportunity, especially those which could be found in upper-level places, threatened continuity of power by attracting able outsiders and opening up avenues of social mobility.

Economic circumstances in Pelham promoted discontinuity. Low-level opportunity encouraged local residents, especially the more able and ambitious ones, to migrate, so no political continuity could be established in that stagnating hilltown. However, since Pelham did not attract many capable outsiders, long-time residents and members of core families were able to retain a modicum of control.

Developments in Ware also encouraged discontinuity. Ware's farmers had neither the skill nor the money necessary to take full advantage of the town's excellent sources of waterpower. That waterpower was very attractive to outsiders who "moved in," built factories, and "took over" the town. Talented, self-confident, and wealthy, the factory owners and their associates seized power in Ware. Nevertheless, population growth in Ware and environs did open new opportunities for local farmers, who retained some limited influence in the town.

Salem's extraordinary commercial opportunities declined sharply during the first quarter of the nineteenth century. Not content with reduced profits, most members of Salem's great commercial families went to Boston or New York where they could find expanding chances for economic gain. This departure left a power vacuum which was filled by long-resident lesser merchants and artisans who were content with the limited opportunities which had driven the great merchants out. Commercially static, Salem's economy did not draw many outsiders who might have threatened the continuing influence of older residents. The peculiar characteristics of Salem's economy also contributed to this process, since artisan trades appear to have been family controlled and the other major areas of her economy demanded substantial capital and were tied to the carrying trade.

Worcester's rapid economic expansion presented many diverse chances for gain—certainly enough to lead many ambitious members of old dominant groups to remain in town. But the remarkable breadth of opportunity in Worcester attracted outsiders and opened the way for substantial entrepreneurial mobility. Both in-migration and mobility disrupted political continuity by creating new sources of potential power.

Northampton's decline in New England's urban hierarchy led some ambitious locals to leave and, coupled with slow, steady economic development, discouraged the entry of outsiders. Nevertheless, the expansion of agriculture kept farm opportunities at a high level, and nonagricultural growth was consistent with both the skills and aspirations of members of long-dominant local families. Such circumstances seem to have been optimal for political continuity.

Economic development further challenged political continuity as local populations increased and diversified. By the 1850s, workingmen without property formed a majority of the adult males in the more developed towns (i.e., all but Pelham). Had these men voted as a bloc for their fellows, they could easily have seized control of their local communities. As we have already seen, most of these men moved with remarkable frequency and probably could not meet residency requirements. Still, they represented a potential source of enormous power. However, the latent possibilities for lower-strata influence came only to a partial and halting realization as the structure of local political processes changed.

In the town-meeting system used in Northampton, Ware, and Pelham, elections were at large—all the town's men chose a clerk and several selectmen. Under the mayor-council system introduced in Worcester (1848) and Salem (1835), the mayor and a half dozen or so aldermen were picked at large, but four councilmen were chosen from each ward with only the residents of the ward voting for them. The town system encouraged election of a few prestigious men, but the shift to ward elections allowed choice of many men and almost immediately led to the selection of artisans and skilled laborers as councilmen.

Under an at-large system during the three years before shifting to city government and ward elections for councilmen, 75% of the men picked in Salem were either merchants or professionals (table 8.6); 42% in Worcester were either merchants or professionals or farmers, and 41.5% were manufacturers. No artisans or skilled laborers were selected during this time. But, in the three years following introduction of a ward system, more than one official in five (Salem, 22%; Worcester, 25%) was a workingman. Later, between 1845 and 1854 under a ward system, Salem voters selected 35% workingmen, and between 1849 and 1854 Worcester citizens picked 33% workingmen.

The full effect of a shift to ward elections and its role in bringing men in new social strata to office can be seen in a comparison of the characteristics of aldermen who were chosen at large and councilmen who were elected by ward. Note again in table 8.7 the high percentage of workingmen chosen as councilmen, the low percentage who were picked as aldermen, and the high proportion of merchants, professionals, and manufacturers elected as aldermen. Had a town system of at-large elections continued, the composition of the board of selectmen would probably have been about like that of the board of aldermen. The change in the structure of elections clearly affected the kind of persons who were chosen, and the change to a ward system brought about a downward shift in the social stratum of officeholders.

The specific occupations of councilmen do not provide many clues as to the reasons for the men's election. It might be expected that persons with wide personal contacts, men engaged in service occupations (storekeepers, grocers, and the like), would be chosen in disproportionate numbers. Such was not the case—rather, no apparent

TABLE 8.6

Occupation, Town-Meeting and Mayor-Council System
(% officeholders in each group)

	At large, town meeting, 1833–1835 (N = 12)	Ward system, mayor-council, 1836–1838 (N = 41)
Salem		
Merchant/professional	75.0	49.0
Manufacturer	0.0	0.0
Business	8.5	20.0
White collar	8.5	7.0
Artisan/skilled labor	0.0	22.0
Unknown	8.5	2.5
	1845–1847 (N = 12)	*1848–1850* (N = 87)
Worcester		
Farm	17.0	16.0
Merchant/professional	25.0	13.0
Manufacturer	41.5	26.0
Business	17.0	11.5
White collar	0.0	7.0
Artisan/skilled labor	0.0	25.0
Unknown	0.0	1.0

pattern appears. Probably persons of influence and power in neighborhood organizations (mechanics' associations, fire companies, etc.) were elected, so occupation itself was not a critical factor.

Though councilmen were drawn from lower social strata than were aldermen and town-meeting officers, they still came from reasonably affluent levels of society. Table 8.8 shows the distribution of aldermen and councilmen for Worcester and Salem in each decile of property owners. More aldermen were drawn from the upper three deciles than were councilmen. Forty-four percent of Worcester's aldermen were from the richest decile alone. More councilmen were unpropertied and came from the lower six deciles. But councilmen were still much more likely to be propertied than was the population at large and, among the propertied, to come from upper social strata. Shift to ward elections lowered the level from which officers were

TABLE 8.7

Occupation of Aldermen and Councilmen (% officeholders in each group)

	Councilmen (by ward) (N = 110)	Aldermen (at large) (N = 35)
Salem (1845–1854)		
Merchant/professional	17.0	34.0
Manufacturer	1.0	3.0
Business	27.0	23.0
White collar	13.0	3.0
Artisan/skilled labor	37.0	26.0
Ship captain	2.0	8.5
Mariner	1.0	3.0
Unknown	2.0	0.0
	(N = 111)	(N = 41)
Worcester (1848–1854)		
Farm	13.5	10.0
Merchant/professional	11.0	22.0
Manufacturer	11.0	27.0
Business	17.0	17.0
White collar	8.0	10.0
Artisan/skilled labor	37.0	15.0
Unknown	2.0	0.0

selected but not so much as to represent a cross-section of the whole population.

Politicization affected officeholding much as did ward elections. That is, when political parties nominated candidates for local office, when they brought extralocal, partisan issues into communal affairs, and when they mobilized voters for local elections, the nature of politics and officeholders changed. Politicization seems to have been primarily a function of hierarchical location and the degree to which members of the community were caught up in the outside world. In Pelham and Ware, outside links were minimal and the level of politicization very low. Ties were stronger in Northampton, yet the local impact of parties was generally limited; but in Worcester and Salem politicization was a critical factor in determining the nature of officeholders.

In Worcester and Salem, parties regularly nominated candidates for city office, but parties do not appear always to have affected local elections. They did not stimulate voters to cast ballots for mayors, councilmen, and aldermen. The reasons for this are many. Since one party consistently won over long periods of time, party competition was not high. Dissident voters who knew that the Whigs "always" swept local offices were not likely to participate in local elections but could be drawn into gubernatorial contests where their vote might be of influence. Parties encouraged this tendency by focusing attention through organized campaigns on general elections in November rather than on local ones in March or December. The timing of these campaigns as well as the issues presented were calculated to pull people into state rather than local contests. Parties thus did not generally touch upon issues which seemed locally relevant—which drew people into political processes at the communal level. For this reason and because of plain indifference, many people simply did not vote.

Table 8.9 shows numbers of voters engaging in state and local elections through the period 1845–1854. Note that during these ten years the state turnout was always higher than local and that, except for 1845 and 1854 in Salem and 1849 in Worcester, the difference was large. However, in Worcester by 1856, after three years of nativist excitement, the gap in participation narrowed to the point where local votes (2,929) actually exceeded gubernatorial ones (2,539). Throughout the period from 1845 to 1860, in both Worcester and Salem, participation in federal elections was roughly consistent with gubernatorial ones, so it would seem that, until the mid-1850s, party politics focused on state and national elections at the expense of local ones.

Table 8.10 shows just how low voter participation was and again stresses the variation between local and state turnouts. The figures represent the percentage of males aged 21 or over who cast a ballot. The low level of overall participation is striking. In 1849 and 1850 in Worcester less than 20% of the potential electorate could control the mayoralty. The figures are even lower for Salem where about 5% could have chosen the mayor in 1850! A higher portion of the populace turned out in state elections, but even at the state level turnout was not high.

Given the small voting base at the local level, it appears possible that well-to-do men continued to dominate local affairs because their potential opponents did not bother to vote. Members of the middle and upper strata could in fact simply have elected themselves. Was this actually the case? Who voted and who did not? Who voted in state elections but not local ones?

Those wards which show lowest participation in both state and local elections show high percentages of common laborers, semiskilled laborers, and, in Salem, sailors. Sailors and unskilled workers do not appear to have voted in any elections. These same low-participation wards had high percentages of young, unattached males—boarders without families—and concentrations of Irishmen. Highly mobile members of these groups may not have met residency qualifications. In any case, they were politically inactive. Higher voter participation

---

TABLE 8.8

Wealth, Aldermen and Councilmen (% officeholders in each decile of property owners)

	N	Richest			
		(1)	(2)	(3)	(4)
Salem (1845–1854)					
Aldermen	35	14	29	34	3
Councilmen	110	8	15	12	7
Worcester (1848–1854)					
Aldermen	41	44	24	2	2
Councilmen	111	16	16	8	10

seems associated with property and upper-status occupations. Greater age and family connection also appear to have contributed to voter participation. Overall, the young, poor, unattached, unskilled, and foreign seem to have been apolitical. Voters were more likely to be family men, propertied, over age 30, and in secure, often upper-status, occupations. Little wonder then that local politics were controlled by members of middle and upper social strata—they were the only ones who voted.

If overall participation shows these relationships, how can the gap between state and local voting be explained? If we assume that young, unattached, unskilled, unpropertied, and Irish men did not vote at all, or at least very infrequently, who voted in state but not local elections? Probably the majority of these voters were skilled laborers, especially younger ones, but no such relationship can be firmly established. Voting and ward data just will not directly prove this connection. However, when skilled workers were drawn into local politics in the nativist outburst of 1854–1856, the level of state participation did not change very much (table 8.11), but the differences between state and local votes tended to disappear. Major increases in local voting came in wards like 3 and 4 in Salem and wards 2, 6, and 7 in Worcester, which had large percentages of skilled laborers. If upper-strata voting remained relatively constant throughout the period 1845–1856, then it may be inferred that skilled workers accounted for the gap; that their participation swung from election to election and was usually drawn more to state politics. Such

(6)	(7)	(8)	(9)	Poorest (10)	Unprop.	Unknown
—	—	—	—	—	6.0	9
1	3	3	1	1.5	25.5	11
—	—	—	2	—	17.0	7
—	1	5	1	—	26.0	7

an argument is consistent with what we know about the composition of nativist groups, which in Worcester, for example, drew almost 80% of their members from among skilled laborers and clerks. The argument is also sustained by the low level of voter increase (i.e., the stability of voting) in high-status areas like wards 8 and 1 in Worcester.

The effects of the participation of skilled workers and of the overall politicization of local elections were substantial. Every person but one who held office in Worcester and Salem in 1853 and 1854 was turned out when nativism and party competition invaded city elections, and the social origins of nativist officeholders were much lower than those of previous officials.

Economic development set in motion other changes which, in the long run, affected the locus and nature of power much more than did ward elections and the politicization of local government. These processes deserve study in their own right but, however important, their analysis is beyond the scope of the present study. The nature and impact of these processes will be only briefly noted in the hope that others will expand upon our very limited description.

As the transportation system grew, as businesses and communities expanded, men engaged in activities and faced problems of increased scale and rising complexity. Present to some degree in all communities, these changes were especially concentrated in large and upper-level places, they decreased in middle-level towns, and they were relatively absent in low-level rural hamlets.

Challenged by new opportunity, men built institutions and administrative organizations to solve problems of scale and complexity. As

TABLE 8.9
Numbers of Voters in State and Local Elections, 1845–1854

	1845	1846	1847	1
Worcester				
Local (mayor)	—	—	—	1
State (gov.)	1,755	1,758	1,677	2
Ratio local/state	—	—	—	
Salem				
Local (mayor)	1,522	1,068	678	1
State (gov.)	1,753	1,490	1,466	2
Ratio local/state	.87	.72	.46	

wells became polluted, aqueduct companies were created. As new buildings went up and crowded together, fires became a serious menace so fire codes were revised and fire companies reorganized. As many young men and women moved through town, as towns expanded in population, the incidence of crime, poverty, and drunkenness increased beyond the capacities of informal means of social control, so poorhouses replaced auctions of the poverty stricken and organized police departments were substituted for vigilante societies. As town governments became more and more unwieldy and expensive, efforts were made to rationalize them and the supposedly more efficient mayor-council system replaced the old "democratic" town meeting.

Primarily concentrated in the larger cities of Worcester and Salem, most of these new institutions and administrative systems were introduced by well-to-do merchants and professional men in consultation with "experts." These experts—men who knew about water systems, schools, fire and police protection, or who "understood" the "causes" of crime, poverty, and insanity—thus gained substantial influence. Knowledge, as the cliché goes, was power. One of the critical changes in patterns of dominance and subordinance was, then, the first tentative emergence of men who used specialized knowledge to press toward influence and power over at least some limited aspect of society. And as this power grew in relation to increasing institutionalization, it signaled the beginning of that process of segmentation so familiar to us in the modern world. As experts gained influence, power also became diffused among many institutions.

Once created, many of the administrative systems began to evolve

9	1850	1851	1852	1853	1854
6	1,751	2,293	1,707	2,173	1,887
•3	2,512	3,031	3,035	3,108	3,072
3	.70	.76	.56	.70	.61
1	478	1,258	1,381	914	1,833
1	2,007	2,272	2,167	2,004	1,989
7	.24	.55	.64	.46	.92

in ways unforeseen by their founders. The founders of city governments certainly never realized the potential effects of ward elections,
nor did the "psychiatrists" ever imagine in their craziest dreams that
their well-intentioned efforts at reform would produce lunatic
asylums where families and communities would lock up their unloved
and unwanted members. Administrative systems—schools, the police

TABLE 8.10

Voter Participation, 1849–1851 (% of
males over age 20 voting in each election)

Worcester	*Ward 1*	*2*	*3*	*4*	*5*	*6*	*7*	*8*	*Total*
1849									
Local	43.0	43.0	35	37.5	30.0	43	36	40.0	38.5
State	60.0	49.0	39	39.0	30.0	51	51	55.0	47.0
1850									
Local	45.0	40.0	31	31.0	28.0	42	39	43.0	37.0
State	62.0	62.0	42	48.0	42.0	56	57	60.0	54.0
1851									
Local	52.5	53.5	36	42.5	35.5	70	45	50.5	49.0
State	69.0	73.0	56	55.0	48.0	68	74	70.5	64.5
Average:									
1849–1851									
Local	47.0	45.5	34	37.0	31.0	50	40	44.5	41.5
State	63.5	61.0	46	47.0	40.0	58	61	62.0	55.0

Salem	*Ward 1*	*2*	*3*	*4*					*Total*
1849									
Local	11.5	27	21.5	25.5					20.5
State	18.0	47	37.5	48.0					36.0
1850									
Local	6.5	15	8.0	11.0					9.5
State	22.0	48	44.5	51.0					40.0
1851									
Local	16.0	34	27.0	27.5					25.0
State	23.5	55	49.0	60.5					46.5
Average:									
1849–1851									
Local	11.5	25	19.0	21.0					18.0
State	21.0	50	44.0	53.0					41.0

TABLE 8.11
Voting in 1853 and 1854 or 1855 (numbers of votes cast in each ward)

Worcester	1	2	3	4	5	6	7	8	Total
1853									
Local	256	261	153	260	286	301	364	292	2,173
State	360	379	238	339	379	465	526	422	3,108
1855									
Local	280	339	182	270	295	401	459	330	2,556
State	374	417	253	344	384	511	630	475	3,388

Salem	1	2	3	4					Total
1853									
Local	150	214	253	297					914
State	275	464	633	632					2,204
1854									
Local	294	373	605	561					1,833
State	285	434	659	611					1,989

and fire departments, city governments, lunatic houses—developed their own rationales and became semiautonomous organizations which possessed power in their own right.

Decentralized, power was thus spread out among several task-centered institutions. Often breaking from the influence and intent of their founders, these administrative systems frequently fell under the control of new social groups or became subject to influences located outside the local community.

Then, too, most of the newly emergent social problems could not be solved at the local level and many of the administrative systems and organizations transcended local boundaries. In both cases, power shifted out of local hands to some higher level of authority. The Massachusetts state government, for example, expanded its control over the police, poorhouses, and schools when it became apparent that the towns would not enforce prohibition laws, care for the transient poor, or properly educate the young.

WHAT HAVE WE learned about power and economic change? Shifts in patterns of political dominance were a function of: (1) the characteristics of dominant groups; (2) the nature of economic change—especially the level and quality of opportunity; (3) the structure of local politics; and (4) the size, complexity, and hierarchical location of local communities. Given the variable influence of these four factors, it would be a mistake to propose any single answer to the question, "What changes took place in patterns of political dominance and subordinance?" It should be apparent by now that the answer depends on where you look.

Indeed, the variability of our findings on political power and social structure points to diversity among American towns and cities and emphasizes the importance of comparative research. Our understanding of American society will only increase as we use a comparative frame of reference. And, if the insights in this book are at all accurate, comparative research which employs central-place and regional economic theory promises to alter fundamentally our conception of the American past.

Appendix

METHODOLOGICAL NOTE

All of the quantitative work in this book has been done by hand without computers or advanced statistical techniques. For the most part, I have worked with whole populations rather than samples. I took all the data from the census or other list and placed it on 3 × 5 cards. Each male aged 16 or over received a card which recorded information about him as well as his parents, wife, and/or children. When a population became so large as to seem unmanageable, I sampled. In these samples, I took information on every second, third, fourth, or tenth person rather than the whole population. In no case have I used less than a 25% sample of the group under study except for priority data in chapter 7.

Doing all the calculations by hand was a severe test of patience (I do not recommend it to others), but it minimized problems of tracing people from one data source to another. In each case, I took all of the evidence from one source and linked that person to another source through all the evidence rather than simply by name. Thus, for example, when using the 1850 and 1860 censuses, I checked a person's name, his age, his wife's name, and the names of his children to be sure that I was dealing with the same person. Idiosyncratic spelling and errors in reporting age made linkage problems more difficult than they might at first seem, especially for Irishmen and single persons, but on the whole I believe few errors were made.

I now realize that my procedures here were not as systematic as they should have been. I drew samples and then discovered that I needed additional data, so I drew other samples. The study is thus based on several different collections of data. I sometimes took material directly from the census and was not as careful as I should have been in recording the number of cases involved or the precise procedures I used. I have also discovered to my horror that my notes on work that I did several years ago are often rather cryptic so, for example, I could not be exactly sure how I had put a table together. Still, despite a certain sloppiness on my part, I believe the data are accurate and representative of "reality." A useful discussion of these problems can be found in the June 1975 issue of the *Historical Methods Newsletter*.

I may have made another error when I excluded women from this book. I did so for several reasons—the major one being the difficulty of linkage owing to marital name changes. I was also certain that women bore little relevance to the themes I wanted to study. I am now somewhat less sure of this than I once was. For example, inclusion of the many female-headed households in early nineteenth-century Salem might have changed wealth distribution in that town to a limited degree. And incorporation of women would surely have increased rates of geographic mobility in towns where large numbers of young women were employed (see my comments in the first few pages of chapter 4). Nevertheless, I am confident that this book's major arguments would not be fundamentally affected by the inclusion of women. After all, women did not own property. They were not formally active in politics and could not vote. Nor is there reason to believe that their patterns of geographic mobility were different from those of males.

Other problems arise in connection with the comparability of information on wealth from one town to another and one epoch to another. Certainly absolute figures for wealth were not comparable from place to place or time to time because assessments were subject to variations created by the assessor. Still, I assume that assessors' biases remained relatively consistent within a town so that distributions of wealth based on assessment were relatively close to distributions of actual property holdings. However, my reading of wills suggests that assessors tended to undervalue large holdings so that actual distributions were undoubtedly more skewed than the assessed distributions which have been used here. Variations between actual and assessed values were probably greatest in larger communities where common public knowledge could not so easily hold discrepancies in check. Nevertheless, I believe that comparison of distributions (but not assessed values) within a single historical epoch gives a reasonably accurate picture of the actual pattern of wealth holding.

The comparability of tax data from one epoch to another is less certain for the assessors may have taken different forms of wealth into account. This does not appear to be the case with real estate assessments which continued to be based on land, building, and other improvements, but the assessment of personal wealth may have shifted (though I can find no evidence of change in the tax laws). However, for two reasons, I do not believe the comparability of wealth data between 1800 and 1860 to be a serious problem: (1) Most changes took place in the distribution of real property and it is here that we can be sure that the assessment base remained relatively constant; and (2) I checked individual tax assessments against total valuations on probate records for Northampton for 1800–1810 and 1850–1860 and the relationship remained relatively constant, with tax assessments generally undervaluing total wealth. In theory, probate valuations represented true wealth and, thus, their base remained stable in 1800–1860, and since tax valuations remained consistent with probate they should be comparable from one time period to another. In no case, however, should the wealth data presented here be equated with more recent evidence on the distribution of income. In that situation two very different things would be compared. On taxation in Massachusetts, see Charles J. Bullock, *Historical Sketch of the Finances and Financial Policy of Massachusetts, 1780–1905* (New York, 1907); and Charles J. Bullock, "Taxation of Property and Income in Massachusetts," *Quarterly Journal of Economics* 31 (1916–1917): 1–61.

DESCRIPTION OF TABLES

Chapter 3

3.1: Data are from federal and state censuses and from Jesse Chickering, *A Statistical View of the Population of Massachusetts from 1765 to 1840* (Boston, 1846).

3.2: Data are from the state census for 1855.

Chapter 4

4.1: Data are from the federal censuses for 1850 and 1860 except for Salem where an 1859 city directory was used in place of the 1860 census. I took adult males from the 1850 census and looked to see if they reappeared in the 1860 census or, in Salem, the 1859 directory. Persons with very common names (e.g., Patrick Murphy) were removed from calculations.

4.2: Data are from the 1850 and 1860 federal censuses. The number of out-migrants was calculated by multiplying the 1850 population by the percentage removed in table 4.1. The number of newcomers was calculated by subtracting out-migrants from the 1850 population and then subtracting the result from the 1860 population.

4.3: Data are from federal censuses for 1850, 1860, and 1800, 1810. I used the same procedure here as with table 4.1. I used an 1859 city directory in place of Salem's 1860 federal census.

4.4: The procedure here is the same as in table 4.2.

4.5: Data are from the 1850 and 1860 federal censuses. The percentages represent that portion of men in each age cohort who did not reappear in the 1860 census. The 1859 city directory was used for Salem.

4.6: The same procedures were used here as in table 4.5 except the cohorts are occupational. The occupational categories are generally self-explanatory, but a few comments are in order. *Business* includes all persons involved in the sale of goods (except those enumerated *merchants*) who appear not to have produced most of the goods with their own labor. *White collar* includes persons in non-manual occupations who worked for others (e.g., clerks). Persons designated laborer, operative, or common laborer were categorized as unskilled *labor*. Those enumerated with specific trades were deemed *skilled laborer/artisan* except for carters, draymen, truckmen, and the like, who were put in the category *semi-skilled*. These occupational categories are relatively traditional, but I increasingly think that they are not particularly useful for analytical purposes. Nevertheless, I have continued to use them here and in chaps. 6 and 7. We need to develop new occupational categories which depart from traditional designations and focus on such matters as the extent to which various occupations adhered to life-cycle expectations, the relationship between age and wealth distribution within and between occupations, and so forth. Such a study deserves a book in its own right and would greatly foster our knowledge about social change and the impact of change on the life chances of nineteenth-century Americans.

4.7: The procedure is the same as in table 4.5 except the cohorts are based upon deciles of real wealth from the 1850 federal census.

4.8: The procedures are the same as in table 4.7 except that only men owning real property are included. The deciles are for propertied men only.

Chapter 5

5.1: Data are from the 1860 federal census of population except for Salem where an 1860 tax valuation was used. I took the aggregate value of real and personal wealth of each adult male and then put each man in rank order from richest to poorest. I then divided this population into ten equal parts (deciles). The figures in the table represent the proportion of the total wealth owned by men in each decile.

5.2: Based on the model described in the text, I assigned an amount of wealth to each adult male based on his age. From this point on, the procedure followed was the same as for table 5.1.

5.3: Based on Northampton federal census for 1860 and local tax valuations for 1800, I assumed anyone paying a "faculty tax" in 1800 was a nonfarmer.

5.4: Data are from federal census for 1860 and Edward Pessen, *Riches, Class, and Power before the Civil War* (Lexington, Mass., 1973), pp. 38–40.

5.5: Data are from federal census for 1860. I calculated decile distributions within each age cohort. The figures in the table represent the proportion of the total wealth within each cohort owned by the richest 10% of the men within that cohort.

5.6: Based on the group criteria outlined in the text, I assigned each adult male to one of the three groups. Young men aged 30 and under have been excluded from calculations.

Chapter 6

6.1: Data are from the 1850 and 1860 federal censuses except for Salem where an 1859 city directory and local tax evaluations were used in the place of the 1860 census. Only males aged 31–60 are included in the calculations.

6.2: See description for table 6.1. Occupations are from the 1850 federal census. See the description of table 4.6 for occupational categories. Only males who improved their real estate holdings by $1,000 or more between 1850 and 1860 are included in the calculations.

6.3: See description for table 6.1. The data base here is all males aged 16 or over who improved their real estate holdings by $1,000 or more.

6.4: See description for table 6.1. Table 6.4 includes only men aged 26 to 35.

6.5: See description for table 6.1. Table 6.5 includes only men aged 41 to 50 who did not own real property in 1850.

6.6: See description for table 6.1. Table 6.6 includes only men aged 31 to 60 who owned real property valued between $750 and $9,999 in 1850.

6.7: See description for table 6.1. Table 6.7 includes only men aged 16 to 60 who owned real property valued at $10,000 or more in 1850.

Chapter 7

7.1: Based on the criteria outlined in chapter 5, I assigned adult males on the 1860 federal census to one of four groups. The figures in table 7.1 represent the percentage of men in each group.

7.2: See description for table 7.1. I traced men in the 1860 samples back to the 1850 federal census. The figures in table 7.2 represent the percentage of men who were present in 1850. I sampled in all towns. I took every tenth adult male in

Salem and Worcester, every third one in Ware and Northampton, and every second one in Pelham.

7.3: The data are from the 1850 and 1860 federal censuses. I calculated net vacancies by taking the 1860 stable population and subtracting the 1850 stable population. I determined total vacancies by adding those created by migration and death to net vacancies.

7.4: See descriptions for tables 7.1–7.3. "Newcomers" were men for whom no priority could be established in 1850. I used samples in each town: Northampton and Ware (33.3%), Salem and Worcester (10%), and Pelham (50%).

Chapter 8

8.1: Names and terms of officeholders come from manuscript town and city records, newspapers, and city directories. Wealth data are for real estate only and are taken from local tax records in 1800 and the federal census for 1850.

8.2: See description for table 8.1.

8.3: See description for table 8.1. Occupational data for 1845–1854 are from the federal census for 1850 and city directories for Worcester and Salem. Occupations for 1800–1809 were difficult to determine. I assumed that 1800–1809 officeholders who did not pay faculty taxes were farmers. Nonfarm occupations came from local histories, genealogies, and the like.

8.4: Data are from the same sources as tables 8.1 and 8.3. I put all officeholders into one of seven occupational categories: farm, merchant, professional, manufacturer, business, white collar, and skilled labor. I then calculated the percentage of the 1845–1854 officeholders who came from categories that had no officeholders between 1800 and 1810.

8.5, 8.6, 8.7, and 8.8: Officeholders can be determined from local newspapers, city directories, and town-meeting records. Occupations and wealth are drawn from the federal census for 1850 and city directories. The deciles in tables 8.7 and 8.8 are based on real estate ownership as revealed in the federal census.

8.9: Election data are from local newspapers. The ratios were calculated by dividing the number of votes cast in elections for mayor by the number of votes cast in elections for governor.

8.10: The percentages were calculated by dividing the number of votes cast by the number of males aged 21 and above in each ward. Data are from local newspapers and the 1850 federal census.

8.11: Voting data are from local newspapers.

Notes

Chapter 1

1. Leo Marx, *Machine in the Garden* (New York, 1964); John William Ward, *Andrew Jackson, Symbol for an Age* (New York, 1962); Marvin Meyers, *Jacksonian Persuasion* (Stanford, 1957).

2. Peter Knights, *The Plain People of Boston* (New York, 1971).

3. The literature on geographic mobility is summarized in Stephan Thernstrom and Peter Knights, "Men in Motion," *Journal of Interdisciplinary History*, Autumn 1970, pp. 7–35. See also Howard Chudacoff, *Mobile Americans* (New York, 1972).

4. Rowland Berthoff, "The American Social Order: A Conservative Hypothesis," *American Historical Review*, April 1960, pp. 495–514.

5. David Rothman, *Discovery of the Asylum in America* (Boston, 1971).

6. Michael Katz, *The Irony of Early School Reform* (Cambridge, Mass., 1968); Raymond Mohl, *Poverty in New York, 1783–1825* (New York, 1971).

7. See, for example, Leonard Richards, *Gentlemen of Property and Standing* (New York, 1970).

8. Edward Pessen, *Riches, Class, and Power before the Civil War* (Lexington, Mass., 1973); Merle Curti, *Making of an American Community* (Stanford, 1959); Stuart Blumin, "Mobility and Change in Ante-Bellum Philadelphia," in Stephan Thernstrom and Richard Sennett, *Nineteenth Century Cities* (New Haven, 1969), pp. 165–208.

9. Pessen, *Riches, Class, and Power*, p. 148.

10. Ibid., pp. 281–306.

11. George M. Frederickson, *The Inner Civil War* (New York, 1965); David Donald, *Lincoln Reconsidered* (New York, 1961); Clifford Griffin, *Their Brothers' Keepers* (New Brunswick, 1960); Robert Dahl, *Who Governs?* (New Haven, 1961).

12. Stephan Thernstrom, *Poverty and Progress* (Cambridge, Mass., 1964).

13. Blumin, "Mobility and Change," in Thernstrom and Sennett, pp. 165–208.

14. Herbert Gutman, "The Reality of the Rags to Riches 'Myth,'" in Thernstrom and Sennett, pp. 98–124.

Chapter 2

1. The histories of the five towns can be followed in: J. R. Trumbull, *History of Northampton* (Northampton, 1902); *The Northampton Book* (Northampton, 1954);

Margaret Pabst, *Agricultural Trends in the Connecticut Valley Region of Massachusetts* (Northampton, 1941); Agnes Hannay, *A Chronicle of Industry on the Mill River* (Northampton, 1936); C. S. Osgood and H. M. Batchelder, *Historical Sketch of Salem* (Salem, 1879); *Essex Institute Historical Collections*, April 1959, on Salem; William Bentley, *Diary*, 4 vols. (Salem, 1905–1914); Sidney Perley, *History of Salem*, 2 vols. (Salem, 1924–1926); Charles Hersey, *History of Worcester, 1836–1861* (Worcester, 1862); William Lincoln, *History of Worcester to 1836* (Worcester, 1862); Arthur Chase, *History of Ware, Massachusetts* (Cambridge, 1911); C. O. Parmenter, *History of Pelham, Massachusetts* (Amherst, 1898). Much of the following general discussion of the towns is taken from these books and also from gazetteers which give basic information about soil, topography, and the like. I have walked the towns, and some of my conclusions are based on these walking tours. My conclusions about the towns' economies are based on general histories and careful study of local tax valuations from the late eighteenth and early nineteenth centuries.

2. Peter Whitney, *History of Worcester* (Worcester, 1793), pp. 27–29.

3. Samuel Eliot Morison, *Maritime History of Massachusetts* (Boston, 1921); James D. Phillips, *Salem in the Indies* (Boston, 1947), and *Salem in the Eighteenth Century* (Boston, 1937).

4. My impressions of family, core, and elite are based on the general histories cited in n. 1 above, random study of family genealogies, and systematic reading of wills probated for each of the towns, 1790–1830. My understanding of the role of family was greatly increased by Bernard Farber's *Guardians of Virtue* (New York, 1972), a provocative study of Salem's families in the late eighteenth century. I have used Farber's ideas throughout the remainder of the chapter.

Chapter 3

1. For general descriptions of this process, see George Rogers Taylor, *The Transportation Revolution* (New York, 1968). Also important are: E. C. Kirkland, *Men, Cities, and Transportation*, vol. 1 (Cambridge, 1948); David Ward, *Cities and Immigrants* (New York, 1971); J. G. Williamson, "Antebellum Urbanization in the American Northeast," *Journal of Economic History* 25 (1965): 592–608; and J. G. Williamson and J. A. Swanson, "The Growth of Cities in the American Northeast, 1820–1920," *Explorations in Entrepreneurial History*, 2nd series, vol. 4 (1966), supplement. Transportation changes in the towns may be followed in: Henry Gere, *Reminiscences of Old Northampton* (Northampton, 1902), p. 41; Worcester city directories for 1829, 1842–1843, 1844–1847; newspaper advertisements in the *Hampshire Gazette* (Northampton), 1837–1850; and the (Worcester) *Daily Spy*, 1828–1845. Materials on transportation and its effects are scattered through the *Collections of the Worcester Society of Antiquity*. See, for example, B. T. Hill, "The Boston and Worcester Railroad," in *Collections* 17 (1901): 527–576. Also useful is Lincoln, *History of Worcester*, pp. 268–269, 281–284, 309–311. My ideas on central place come from Kirkland's *Men, Cities, and Transportation* and M. H. Yeates and B. J. Garner, *North American Cities* (New York, 1971). Ron Tobey's article on central place, "How Urbane Is the Urbanite?" *Historical Methods Newsletter*, Sept. 1974, pp. 259–275, appeared too late for incorporation into this study but should be consulted.

2. Pabst, *Agricultural Trends in the Connecticut Valley Region*. I also analyzed the 1850 and 1860 federal censuses of agriculture for each of the five towns.

3. My ideas about internal urban structure come from gazetteers and general descriptions of the towns as well as analysis of maps which include the location of industry. I took maps of Salem and Worcester and stuck colored and numbered pins in them in order to discover where different kinds of firms were located and where different sorts of people lived. I also used an 1850 Worcester street list.

4. Ward data are from the federal census population schedules from 1850.

Chapter 4

1. See Thernstrom and Knights, "Men in Motion," pp. 7–35; and Knights, *Plain People of Boston*.

2. Many of the ideas here were initially suggested to me by Stephan Thernstrom.

3. I calculated maximum turnover in Worcester and Salem by comparing all the males listed in the 1850 city directories with those listed in the 1851 directories.

4. On the Lincoln family, see Charles Nutt, *History of Worcester* (New York, 1919), 1: 169–178.

5. Sidney Goldstein discusses this duality of population in his "Repeated Migration as a Factor in High Mobility Rates," *American Sociological Review* 19 (Oct. 1954): 536–541.

6. Richard Jensen first pointed out to me the potential connections among life cycle, wealth distribution, and geographic mobility in his comments on a paper I presented at the 1970 Brockport Conference on Social History, entitled "Property Distribution in Jacksonian America."

7. I analyzed the moves of 256 men listed in Charles Nutt, *History of Worcester*, vols. 3 and 4. The highly subjective data in the Nutt biographies were not easily subject to quantification, so my conclusions here should be deemed impressionistic, but I am confident of their overall accuracy.

8. On Washburn, see Joshua Chasan, "Civilizing Worcester: The Creation of Institutional and Cultural Order in Worcester, Massachusetts, 1848–1876" (Ph.D. thesis, University of Pittsburgh, 1974).

Chapter 5

1. See Lee Soltow, *Men and Wealth in the United States, 1850–1870* (New Haven, 1975), p. 93.

2. The idea for the $200 model was first suggested to me by Richard Jensen. See also chap. 2 and 3 in Soltow's *Men and Wealth*.

3. Soltow, *Men and Wealth*, p. 72.

4. Generalizations here are based on an analysis of the federal censuses of agriculture and manufacture for 1850 and 1860. Data on the Ware mills are from the 1860 manufacturing census. The wealth figure for Gilbert and Stevens comes from the 1860 federal census of population.

5. Soltow, *Men and Wealth*, p. 41.

6. James Henretta, "Economic Development and Social Structure in Colonial Boston," *William and Mary Quarterly*, 3rd series, 22 (1965): 75–92. See also Jackson T. Main, *Social Structure of Revolutionary America* (Princeton, 1965), and Soltow, *Men and Wealth*, p. 108.

7. Pessen, *Riches, Class, and Power*, pp. 38–40; Blumin, "Mobility and Change," in Thernstrom and Sennett, pp. 165–208.

Chapter 6

1. Stephan Thernstrom's two books, *Poverty and Progress* and *The Other Bostonians* (Cambridge, 1973), provide a good introduction to the literature on social mobility.

2. Most of my data here come from local histories and genealogies, so my conclusions are quite impressionistic.

3. These processes in Worcester may be followed in Charles Washburn, *Industrial Worcester* (Worcester, 1917); and in the biographies in Nutt, *History of Worcester*. Chasan's "Civilizing Worcester" should also be consulted.

4. I traced all men valued over $9,999 real estate from the 1860 federal population census back to the 1850 census in each of the five towns.

Chapter 7

1. The ideas here on priority were initially suggested to me by Walter Glazer of the University of Pittsburgh history department. See his study, "Participation and Power: Voluntary Associations and Functional Organizations in Cincinnati in 1840," *Historical Methods Newsletter*, Sept. 1972, pp. 151–168.

Chapter 8

1. The literature on community power is conveniently summarized in W. D. Hawley and James H. Svara, *The Study of Community Power* (Santa Barbara, 1972). Data for chap. 8 came from manuscript town-meeting and city-government records, city directories, local newspapers, tax records, and the federal population census for 1850. Priority data came from birth records, other genealogical material, and city directories.

2. I traced family and priority in Salem and Worcester through city directories and published birth, death, and marriage records. In Northampton, Ware, and Pelham, I used many sources: manuscript birth and marriage records, local histories, gazetteers, and genealogies were particularly useful. Manuscript materials are in the possession of the town and city clerks, but important manuscript and published materials can be found in the Forbes Library in Northampton.

Index

Northampton, Massachusetts: core and elite in, 16–17; and economic change, 20–21, 23, 24; in 1800, 11–12; geographic mobility in, 30, 45; group sizes in, 70–72; political power in, 82–92; population change in, 25–29; property mobility in, 56–69; vacancies in, 72–77; wealth distribution in, 46–55

Occupation: categories of, 105; and elections by ward, 92–95; and office-holding, 84–87; and property mobility, 60–61

Patriarchal communities, 15; conflict with atomistic conception of society, 44–45

Pelham, Massachusetts: core and elite in, 15–16; and economic change, 20, 23; in 1800, 10; geographic mobility in, 30–45; group sizes in, 70–72; political power in, 82–92; population decline in, 25–29; property mobility in, 56–69; vacancies in, 72–77; wealth distribution in, 46–55

Persistence of adult males, 30–31

Pessen, Edward, 5, 6, 8, 52

Political power, 6–7, 14–18, 82–102

Politicization, effect of, on local office-holding, 95–98

Priority, 71–72; and officeholding, 87–89

Property mobility, 56–59; levels of, 60–61; and occupation, 60

Rothman, David, 5

Salem, Massachusetts: core and elite in, 15, 17–18; and economic change, 22; in 1800, 12–14; geographic mobility in, 30–45; group sizes in, 70–72; political power in, 82–102; population change in, 25–29; property mobility in, 56–69; vacancies in, 72–77; wealth distribution in, 46–55

Social (vertical) mobility, 7–8

Social model, 56–58, 70–72

Soltow, Lee, 47, 51

Spinoff (economic), 68, 79; importance of, in Northampton, 24; in Salem, 25; in Ware, 23; in Worcester, 22–23

Stable population, 37–40, 43–44, 56–58, 70–72, 79–80; vacancies in, 72–77

Successful men (climbers), definition of, 59

Tables, description of, 105–7

Thernstrom, Stephan, 4, 7, 8, 111 n

Tocqueville, Alexis de, 2–3

Tracking, 74–77

Transients, 3–4, 39–40, 44, 56–58

Urban hierarchy: changes in, from 1800–1860, 19–25; effects of, 75–79; in 1800, 14; and the five towns, 20; and geographic mobility, 32; and social structure, 56–58, 70–72; and wealth distribution, 52–55

Vacancies in the stable population, 72–77

Ward elections: effects of, 92–95; and multicentered communities, 29

Ward, John William, 3

Ware, Massachusetts: core and elite in, 15–16; and economic change, 23–24; in 1800, 10; geographic mobility in, 30–45; group sizes in, 70–72; political power in, 82–92; population change in, 25–29; property mobility in, 56–69; vacancies in, 72–77; wealth distribution in, 46–55

Warning out, 35

Wealth and officeholding, 82–84, 94–95

Wealth distribution, 5–6, 46–55; and age, 53–55; and economic activity, 50–53; and the urban hierarchy, 52–55

Worcester, Massachusetts: core and elite in, 16–17; and economic change, 19–20, 22–23, 24–25; in 1800, 11–12; geographic mobility in, 30–45; group sizes in, 70–72; political power in, 82–102; population change in, 25–29; property mobility in, 56–69; vacancies in, 72–77; wealth distribution in, 46–55

Young men (as a social group), 49, 56–58; and priority, 71–72; property mobility among, 62–63

Library of Congress Cataloging in Publication Data

Doherty, Robert W.

Society and power.

Includes bibliographical references and index.

1. Cities and towns—Massachusetts—History.

2. New England—Social conditions.   I.   Title.

HN79.M4D64   309.1'74   77-73477

ISBN 0-87023-242-8